W9-CKQ-534

THE TUSKEGEE AIRMEN, AN ILLUSTRATED HISTORY

Tuskegee Airmen in one of the flight formations that would soon carry them over enemy territory. Here they are flying the shark-nosed P-40 fighter aircraft on a 1943 practice mission from Selfridge Field, Michigan.

The Tuskegee Airmen, An Illustrated History 1939-1949

JOSEPH CAVER

JEROME ENNELS

DANIEL HAULMAN

NEWSOUTH BOOKS
Montgomery | Louisville

NewSouth Books
105 South Court Street
Montgomery, AL 36104

Library of Congress Cataloging-in-Publication Data

Caver, Joseph.
The Tuskegee airmen : an illustrated history, 1939-1949 / Joseph Caver, Jerome
Ennels, Daniel Haulman.

p. cm.

Includes bibliographical references and index.

ISBN-13: 978-1-58838-244-3
ISBN-10: 1-58838-244-3

1. United States. Army Air Forces. Fighter Group, 332nd—History. 2. United
States. Army Air Forces. Fighter Squadron, 99th—History. 3. United States.
Army Air Forces. Composite Group, 477th—History. 4. United States. Army Air
Forces—African American troops. 5. African American pilots—History—20th
century. 6. World War, 1939-1945—Participation, African American. 7. World
War, 1939-1945—Aerial operations, American. 8. World War, 1939-1945—
Campaigns—Western Front. I. Ennels, Jerome, 1950- II. Haulman, Daniel L.
(Daniel Lee), 1949- III. Title.
D790.252332nd .C37 2011
940.54'4973cdc22

2011011463

Design by Randall Williams.

Printed in the United States of America by Malloy, Inc., Ann Arbor, Michigan.

TO THE TUSKEGEE AIRMEN

Contents

Foreword

Roscoe Brown Jr.

Captain, USAAF, 100th Fighter Squadron, 332nd Fighter Group

When I was flying combat missions with the Tuskegee Airmen over Germany and enemy-held territory more than sixty-five years ago, I never imagined that we were making history.

It is often said that the Tuskegee Airmen "changed the world" by successfully challenging the stereotypes that suggested that African Americans did not possess the skills, intelligence, or courage to become military pilots. This stereotype was broken in March 1942 when the first class of five graduated from the Tuskegee Flying Training Program. As history records, the 332nd Fighter Group—the famed "Red Tails"—compiled an unusually impressive record while flying bomber escort and ground support missions.

Joseph Caver, Jerome Ennels, and Daniel Haulman have done an exceedingly thorough analysis of the chronological history of the experiences and exploits of the Tuskegee Airmen, which includes not only the fighter and bomber pilots, but also the ground support officers and enlisted personnel—totaling many thousands.

By examining in detail the orders, mission reports, citations, and official pronouncements related to the Tuskegee Airmen, the authors have presented a real-life history of this remarkable episode in military and social history. In reviewing the chronology, I found myself reminiscing about the missions and the challenges we faced in overcoming the obstacles that we encountered.

I commend this book to all who want to explore and understand the accomplishments of this pioneer group of black airmen. On behalf of my fellow Tuskegee Airmen, I would like to express my gratitude to the authors for such an outstanding effort to preserve our history and acknowledge our contributions.

Dr. Roscoe Brown was among the original Tuskegee Airmen. He served with distinction in the European Theater and is one of three Tuskegee Airmen who downed German Me-262 jets, an especially remarkable feat because the American pilots were flying slower P-51 propeller-driven fighters.

TUSKEGEE AIRMEN STATISTICS

14,600 plus individuals in the various Tuskegee Airmen organizations in World War II, including pilots and ground personnel.

992 pilots trained at Tuskegee Army Air Field (673 single engine, 252 twin engine, 51 liaison, 11 service, and 5 Haitian).

989 plus missions of the 99th, 100th, 301st, and 302nd Fighter Squadrons for the Twelfth Air Force.

500 missions of the 99th Fighter Squadron by early June 1944.

311 plus missions of the 332nd Fighter Group for the Fifteenth Air Force (June 1944– May 1945).

179 bomber escort missions of the 332nd Fighter Group for Fifteenth Air Force.

172 heavy bomber escort missions of the 332nd Fighter Group for Fifteenth Air Force.

112 aerial victories of the 99th Fighter Squadron and the 332nd Fighter Group combined during World War II.

96 Distinguished Flying Crosses awarded to members of the 332nd Fighter Group or its squadrons.

94 aerial victories of the 332nd Fighter Group for the Fifteenth Air Force between June 1944 and the end of April 1945.

61 missions under the Fifteenth Air Force for which the 332nd Fighter Group reported one or more of its own aircraft lost or missing.

51 liaison pilot graduates from Tuskegee Army Air Field.

46 average number of bombers shot down by enemy aircraft for each of the other six fighter groups of the Fifteenth Air Force.

44 classes of military pilots graduated at Tuskegee Army Air Field.

35 missions in which the 332nd Fighter Group reported enemy aircraft encounters.

27 bombers shot down by enemy aircraft when those bombers were in groups the 332nd Fighter Group was assigned to escort.

25 332nd Fighter Group missions for the Fifteenth Air Force on which its members reported seeing bombers go down (some of these were bombers not assigned to the 332nd Fighter Group to escort).

21 additional missions in which the 332nd Fighter Group reported seeing enemy aircraft but had no encounters with them.

21 332nd Fighter Group missions for the Fifteenth Air Force in which Tuskegee Airmen shot down enemy aircraft.

18 aerial victories earned by the 99th Fighter Squadron before it joined the 332nd Fighter Group.

7 missions of the 332nd Fighter Group for the Fifteenth Air Force on which bombers under escort were lost to enemy aircraft.

5 Haitian pilot graduates at Tuskegee Army Air Field.

4 highest number of aerial victories by a Tuskegee Airman (by Lee Archer, Joseph Elsberry, and Edward Toppins).

4 types of aircraft Tuskegee Airmen flew in combat (P-40s, -39s, -47s, and -51s).

4 Tuskegee Airmen with three aerial victories in one day (Joseph Elsberry, Clarence Lester, Lee Archer, and Harry Stewart).

3 German jets shot down by Tuskegee Airmen.

3 Distinguished Unit Citations earned by Tuskegee Airmen organizations (99th Fighter Squadron earned two before it was assigned to the 332nd Fighter Group, and the 332nd Fighter Group earned one after the 99th was assigned to it).

THE TUSKEGEE AIRMEN,
AN ILLUSTRATED HISTORY

AVIATRIX MUST SIGN AWAY LIFE TO LEARN TRADE

"If I can create the minimum of my plans and desires there shall be no regrets."

— Elizabeth "Bessie" Coleman (1892–1926)

Miss Bessie Coleman Walked Nine Miles Each Day While Studying Aviation

Miss Bessie Coleman, 4533 Indiana avenue, the only feminine aviatrix of the Race in the world, arrived in Chicago Saturday direct from France where she has just completed a ten months' course in aviating.

Miss Coleman was seen by a Defender reporter at her home. When asked why she took up the game of flying, she said:

"Well, because I knew we had no aviators, neither men nor women, and I knew the Race needed to be represented along this most important line, so I thought it my duty to

INTRODUCTION

JOSEPH CAVER, JEROME ENNELS, AND DANIEL HAULMAN

During the early twentieth century, many white military and civilian aviation experts were convinced that African Americans "lacked the mental capacity, aptitude, and reflexes" to fly airplanes. In fact, official studies done by the Army War College in the 1920s and 1930s concluded that blacks were a "mentally inferior subspecies of the human race" with "smaller brains that weighed ten ounces less than those of whites." These studies also rationalized that the few blacks who had become pilots were exceptions to the general rule and usually possessed a high percentage of white blood. In short, the general feeling was that blacks were overwhelmed by aviation technology and inherently afraid of flying.

Nothing was further from the truth. In fact, even before the turn of the century, black men had mastered many of the technological aspects of flight and demonstrated no fear of the inherent dangers associated with even the earliest attempts to fly. By 1899, John F. Pickering of Gonaives, Haiti, had submitted a design to the U.S. Patent Office for a steerable balloon. Another black man, Charles Wesley Peters of Pittsburgh, constructed a number of kites and gliders and at age fourteen successfully made his first glider flight. Later in 1911, less than

ten years after the Wright brothers' first successful powered flight at Kitty Hawk, North Carolina, Walter E. Swagerty, a black San Franciscan, designed a flying machine, learned to fly it, and appeared at county fairs throughout the Southwest. In other words, "whites did not have a monopoly on flying aptitude," and blacks shared the same interest in and commitment to the "angelic" art of flight.

Black women were also among the early pioneers of flight. Elizabeth "Bessie" Coleman, for example, was one of the first black female aviators. Refused admission to several flying schools in the United States, Coleman went to Europe in 1921 where she obtained a license from the Federation Aeronautique Internationale. As a result, she was the first black female to obtain a pilot's license and the first of her race and gender to hold an international pilot's license. On September 22, 1922, Coleman performed in her first American air show at Curtis Field near Manhattan and later participated in numerous exhibition flights all over the country. Flying primarily in a Curtis JN-4D, her hair-raising daredevil stunts earned her the nickname of "Brave Bessie," and her aerial demonstration performances soon became legendary. By her death in April 1926, "Brave Bessie" had become

Coleman

Banning

Bullard

one of America's most popular stunt flyers.

During the same period, Hubert Julian, a flamboyant young black aviator from the West Indies, moved to the United States. Nicknamed the "Black Eagle of Harlem," he claimed that the Canadian war ace Billy Bishop had taught him to fly, and he quickly gained a reputation as a skilled pilot. In July 1924, Julian attempted to become the first person to make a solo trans-Atlantic flight from New York to Africa, but he crashed his airplane, "The Ethiopia I," into the Atlantic shortly after takeoff. He spent several weeks in the hospital recovering from his injuries. Although he was beaten across the Atlantic by Charles Lindbergh, in 1929 Bishop completed his trans-Atlantic flight.

Black aviators were also among the earliest fliers involved in trans-continental flights. In February 1927, Joel Ace and his mechanic Artis Ward left Los Angeles in an old patched-up Curtis JN-4 "Jenny" en-route to New York City. However, engine troubles forced them down in Salt Lake City, where they spent several weeks trying to repair the engine. Later, with the engine finally up and running, they eventually made it to Chicago before additional mechanical problems caused them to abort their flight entirely. Two years later, Julian became one of America's first black flyers to fly coast to coast. Three years passed before two other black men, James Banning and Thomas Allen, also completed a coast-to-coast flight across the United States. The two aviators flew from Los Angeles to Long Island in a plane pieced together largely from junkyard parts. They made the 3,300-mile journey in less than forty-two hours of flying time.

Equally as impressive was the Pan-American Goodwill Flight. In an airplane christened the "Booker T. Washington," Charles Alfred Anderson and Dr. Albert E. Forsythe left Atlantic City on November 8, 1934. Anderson, who had taught himself to fly, was one of the first blacks in the country to earn a private license and to qualify as a transport pilot. Forsythe, on the other hand, was a graduate of Tuskegee Institute and later earned a medical degree from McGill University in Montreal. The previous year, the two aviators had completed a round-trip trans-continental flight followed by a round-trip flight from Atlantic City to Montreal.

The Pan-American flight was to last thirty days, cover more than twelve thousand miles, and include visits to more than twenty countries. But shortly after completing the Caribbean phase of the journey, their airplane stalled and crashed, bringing the tour to an untimely end.

IN 1939, CHAUNCEY SPENCER and Dale White conducted a ten-stop cross country demonstration flight from Chicago to Washington, then to New York and back to Chicago, not only to demonstrate the ability of black men to fly, but also to increase their opportunities to do so. Sponsored by the National Airmen's Association, their flight was publicized in the *Chicago Defender* newspaper and other black press. In Washington, Spencer and White met with certain congressmen. The flight might have contributed to the passage, that same year of the Civilian Pilot Training Act that included a provision banning racial discrimination in the program. Spencer and White claimed to have met Congressman Everett Dirksen of their home state of Illinois and Harry S. Truman of Missouri. Truman was destined to become the Democratic president whose post-World War II executive order ended racial segregation in the military services, and Dirksen became one of the key Republican supporters of the Civil Rights Act of 1964.

The Civilian Pilot Training (CPT) Act of 1939 authorized the creation of several hundred flight training facilities at colleges across the country. After the passage of the legislation, black Ameri-

Hubert Julian promoted his achievements as a pioneering black aviator in a barnstorming aerial "circus."

James Banning and Thomas Allen built a plane from spare parts and flew it cross-country.

cans began sending President Franklin D. Roosevelt requests to allow them to enroll in the pilot training program. Historically black Wilberforce University, Hampton Institute, and Tuskegee Institute offered their campuses for pilot training. By the end of 1939, nearly ten thousand students were enrolled in the CPT programs at more than five hundred colleges and vocational schools. A few black students enrolled in CPT at predominantly white colleges in the Northeast and Midwest, and hundreds more enrolled at historically black Hampton Institute, Howard University, North Carolina A&T, Delaware State College, West Virginia State College, and Tuskegee Institute.

On October 15, 1939, Tuskegee Institute received its certificate from the Civil Aeronautical Authority. Tuskegee efforts to obtain the charter were led by President Frederick D. Patterson and George L. Washington. Under the leadership of Tuskegee's Chief Pilot Charles A. Anderson, more than a hundred students graduated from the CPT program. Many of the CPT graduates would find their way to the Tuskegee Army Flying School when it opened in 1941.

DESPITE THEIR MANY AERIAL successes in civilian aviation, early attempts by blacks to enter the American military aviation arena during World War I had been blocked by white civilian and military aviation officials. Many of them continued to argue that blacks were cowardly under combat conditions and would never have what it took to fly and fight in military aircraft.

Corporal Eugene Jacques Bullard's efforts to join the American Air Service had been unsuccessful even though he was a proven and highly decorated

Eugene Bullard flew for the French during World War I and was the first black aviator to shoot down an enemy plane.

combat veteran of World War I in which he served as a pilot in the French Air Force. Born in Columbus, Georgia, in October 1894, Bullard left home at age eleven and traveled as a stowaway to France. When World War I started, he enlisted in the French Foreign Legion and rose to the rank of corporal. He later accepted an offer to join the French Air Force, and, after completing training, joined two hundred other American pilots in the Lafayette Flying Corps. While flying combat missions from August 27 to November 11, 1918, Bullard distinguished himself, becoming the first black military pilot to destroy an enemy aircraft in combat. He shot down at least one German aircraft (his claim of a second kill was never confirmed).

Years later, when Fascist Italy invaded Ethiopia

in 1935, Hubert Julian volunteered his services in defense of the African country. After commissioning him as a colonel in the Ethiopian military, Emperor Haile Selassie put Julian in charge of the small Ethiopian Air Force. His career with the Ethiopian Air Force, however, was short-lived following an altercation with fellow black American aviator John C. Robinson. Shortly after the incident with Robinson, who had also been commissioned as a colonel in the Ethiopian Air Force, the Emperor ordered Julian to leave the country.

Following Julian's departure, Selassie made Robinson commander of the Ethiopian Air Force. Known as the "Brown Condor," Robinson helped

John C. Robinson, an alumnus of Tuskegee Institute, became commander of the Ethiopian Air Force.

to establish the country's fledgling air force and actively participated in a reconnaissance mission for the Ethiopian Army. Flying through dangerous and unfamiliar airspace from Addis to Adwa and back, Robinson carried critical supplies, Ethiopian fighters, and even the emperor himself to various destinations during the peak of the conflict. Numerous efforts to shoot him down were unsuccessful, and he returned to the United States as a genuine African American war hero. He returned to Ethiopia after the war as the head of an African American team of aviators and technicians to help Ethiopia build a modern air force.

Despite the accomplishments of Bullard, Julian, and Robinson, the doors to U.S. military aviation remained closed to men of color. Those doors finally opened on November 8, 1941, when the first class of black aviation cadets began primary flying training in Tuskegee, Alabama. On March 7, 1942, five members of the first class of black flying students graduated from advanced flying training at Tuskegee Army Air Field and became the nation's first black military pilots. By the end of World War II, nearly a thousand black men had earned their wings at Tuskegee and had gone on to chalk up one of the most impressive aerial combat records in the history of American military aviation.

Despite the achievements and extraordinary efforts of black aviators and their supporters before World War II, opportunities in aviation for most African Ameri-

Willa Beatrice Brown served her country in the U.S. Civil Air Patrol and as an outspoken advocate for African American aviators.

cans were few before the Tuskegee Airmen, a point argued by Willa B. Brown to none other than First Lady Eleanor Roosevelt (see letter, page 22). Brown was the first black woman to receive a commission as a lieutenant in the U.S. Civil Air Patrol. She was also president of the National Airmen's Association of America. In 1939, she had successfully lobbied for federal funds to support the Chicago-based National Airmen's Association pilot training program, the Coffey School of Aviation, which was the first privately run training school for black pilots in the country.

Nonetheless, there were precious few civilian African American pilots and none at all in the U.S. military before the first graduating class of Tuskegee Airmen at Tuskegee Army Air Field. The accomplishment of these pilots and their successors in the various Tuskegee Airmen organizations finally opened the door.

HOWEVER, WHETHER THE BLACK pilots would enter combat was still an open question. The Army Air Forces allowed the 99th Fighter Squadron, the first African American flying unit, to deploy to North Africa in the spring of 1943, but at first they were limited to flying patrols along the coast and over shipping in the area. The pilots of the 99th flew P-40 aircraft of the same type with which they had practiced at Tuskegee for transition flying training after advanced training in T-6s.

Even after the 99th Fighter Squadron participated in combat operations in the Mediterranean Theater, its right to remain in combat came into question. The 99th Fighter Squadron was not assigned to any

NATIONAL AIRMEN'S ASSOCIATION OF AMERICA

"THE PIONEER BRANCH"

3435 INDIANA AVENUE
CHICAGO, ILLINOIS

President
WILLA B. BROWN

1st Vice President
A MANSFIELD BRIGHT

2nd Vice President
CORNELIUS R. COFFEY

Secretary
JOY GURLEY

Assistant Secretary
RACHEL L. CARTER

Treasurer
ALBERT P. STUMP

Business Manager
NEAL SIMEON

Publicity Agent
SIMEON E. BROWN

Historian
OTIS GRANT COLLINS

Sergeant-at-Arms
GEORGE WEBSTER

Adviser
ENOC P. WATERS, JR.

December 6, 1941

Mrs. Franklin D. Roosevelt
White House
Washington, D. C.

Dear Mrs. Roosevelt:

It has been with deep admiration that I have followed your interest in the women of our country and especially your message to Negro women recently in which you stated, "As Negro women, you have a vital part to play in the Civilian Defense Program". These words of yours made me and many, many other members of my race very happy.

I am a young Negro woman and have already spent three years sponsoring civilian defense of our country acting as Federal Coordinator of two units of the Civilian Pilot Training Program, and as organizer and promoter of the National Airmen's Association of America which is composed chiefly of Negro pilots throughout the United States. In addition, I helped to organize and was elected vice-president of the Aeronautical Association of Negro Schools. Enclosed with this letter you will find clippings from newspapers which, rather thoroughly, describe the type of work which I am doing. I hope you will find time to glance at them. During the past three years I have devoted full time to aviation, and for the most part marked progress has been made, and at the suggestion of Mrs. Crystal Bird Fauset, my associations are lending full strength to the U. S. Office of Civilian Defense.

I have, however, encountered several difficulties -- several of them I have handled very well, and some have been far too great for me to master. I would like to talk with you some time if you can spare a few minutes when you are passing through Chicago, or, if it would please you better, sometime when you are at home in Washington. I come in and out of Washington quite often.

You may rest assured that any time spent in the interest of my aviation associations will be well appreciated.

Sincerely yours

Willa B. Brown

Willa B. Brown
President

WBB/lig

William J. Powell was another passionate advocate for early black aviation. Above, heavyweight boxing champion Joe Louis *(second from left)* visits Powell *(right)* in Los Angeles at the workshop of the Bessie Coleman Aero Club, which Powell founded. An engineering graduate, he enlisted in officer training school and served in a segregated Army unit during World War I. A successful businessman after the war, he became interested in aviation and moved to California to learn to fly. At left is an advertisement for *Black Wings*, a book he wrote to encourage blacks to seek careers in aviation.

white fighter group. Rather, it was attached to different groups at various times, and the commanders of those groups had different opinions about the flying ability of black men. One of the commanders complained that the 99th Fighter Squadron was not performing as well as the white fighter squadrons and should be taken out of combat. In response, the Army Air Forces launched a study to compare the performance of the 99th with the other P-40 squadrons in Twelfth Air Force. That study concluded that the 99th Fighter Squadron was performing as well as the white P-40 squadrons with which it served.

The success of the 99th Fighter Squadron in combat, first in North Africa and later in Sicily and the mainland of Italy, assured that other African American fighters squadrons, the 100th, 301st, and 302nd, would also get to deploy and enter combat. The latter three squadrons belonged to the 332nd Fighter Group. After the 332nd deployed to Italy in January 1944, it flew P-39s on the same kind of tactical patrol missions that the 99th Fighter Squadron was flying with P-40s, but at first the 99th was not assigned to the 332nd Fighter Group. Neither the P-39 nor the P-40 was well-suited for air-to-air combat, and neither the 99th Fighter Squadron nor the

332nd Fighter Group at first achieved many aerial victories in comparison to white fighter groups that flew P-47 or P-51 aircraft, which were much faster and more maneuverable.

After the 332nd Fighter Group was reassigned from the Twelfth to the Fifteenth Air Force, it began to fly first P-47 and then P-51 fighters, which were the best American fighters in the war because of their speed and range. Escorting heavy bombers such as B-17 Flying Fortresses and B-24 Liberators to targets deep within German-held territory gave the Tuskegee Airmen pilots more opportunity, not only to shoot down enemy aircraft but also to prove that they could fly any fighter mission the Army Air Forces could offer. In fact the Tuskegee Airmen flew those bomber escort missions so well that some observers thought they were even better than the other fighter groups in the Fifteenth Air Force. The claim that the Tuskegee Airmen "never lost a bomber" was not accurate, but the claim itself reflected the high regard in which the black aviators were held. Opportunity was a two-edged sword. The chance to fly missions deep into Germany also meant the chance to lose pilots on those missions, and many were shot down. Some survived months in German prisoner-of-war camps.

The success of the 99th Fighter Squadron not only paved the way for the 332nd Fighter Group and the 100th, 301st, and 302nd Fighter Squadrons to enter combat, but also for the training of black pilots to fly multi-engine bombers. When the 332nd Fighter Group deployed from Selfridge Field, Michigan, to Italy, the 477th Bombardment Group was activated at Selfridge. It was the first and only African American bomber group in the Army Air Forces, and it trained with B-25 medium bombers at bases in Michigan, Kentucky, and Indiana.

Although it never deployed overseas and never entered combat, the 477th Bombardment Group further extended aviation opportunity for African Americans. Not only did it prepare bomber pilots in a field from which they had been excluded, it also struck a powerful blow against segregation in the U.S. armed forces. When the white commander of the 477th tried to enforce segregated officers' clubs at Freeman Field, many of the black pilots, navigators, and bombardiers refused to obey an order. They were arrested, and the group was transferred back to Godman Field after what became known as the "Freeman Field Mutiny." The resistance of 477th Bombardment Group members to racial segregation at Freeman resulted in their eventual exoneration, and the Army Air Forces had to enforce its own regulations against such segregation on U.S. military bases.

Just as the 332nd Fighter Group and its four squadrons demonstrated that black pilots could do all the tasks that white pilots could do with fighters in combat, the 477th Bombardment Group proved that black pilots could fly multi-engine bombers, and that they would not tolerate a roll-back on the little racial integration that had been achieved by 1945.

The Tuskegee Airmen opened the door of opportunity for blacks in aviation wider than it had ever been opened before. After them, black men could not only be military pilots, they could also fly any kind of fighter in the Army Air Forces inventory. They could also fly bombers, with bombardiers and navigators. Finally, the success of the Tuskegee Airmen in combat—and in resistance at home to segregationist policies—contributed immeasurably to the ultimate integration of the U.S. armed forces. It is not surprising that racial segregation in the American armed forces ended around the same time that the United States Air Force was born.

≡ *Part 1* ≡

TRAINING

Civilian Pilot Training

Primary Flying Training

Basic Flying Training

Advanced Flying Training

Training Beyond Tuskegee

Above: Old Moton Field was used by Tuskegee Institute for its Civilian Pilot Training. Today it is the Tuskegee Airmen National Historic Site.

Below: Prior to the opening of Moton Field, members of Tuskegee Institute's first CPT class made an 80-mile round trip to Gunter Field for training. Gunter opened in 1930 as Montgomery's first municipal airport, before becoming Gunter Army Air Field in 1940. Later it was Gunter Air Force Station and today is the Gunter Annex of Maxwell Air Force Base.

1

CIVILIAN PILOT TRAINING

As World War II loomed, several European countries began training thousands of young civilians to become pilots. In spite of what they were being called, these government-sponsored activities were for all practical purposes military flight training programs. The United States quickly followed suit and passed the Civil Aeronautics Act of 1938, which authorized funding for a trial program that became known as the Civilian Pilot Training Program (CPTP). Unveiled by President Franklin D. Roosevelt on December 27, 1938, the program's goal was to train 20,000 college students a year as civilian pilots.

The first students entered the program in early 1939 at eleven colleges and universities across the United States. Other schools were later added. Among them were several black educational institutions, namely Tuskegee Institute, Hampton Institute, Virginia State University, and Howard University. These schools would become instrumental in opening the doors for the first African American military pilots to enter the Army Air Corps.*

Following the attack on Pearl Harbor and the American entry into World War II, the Civilian Pilot Training Program became known as the War Training Service (WTS). From 1942 to 1944, the WTS served primarily as the screening program for potential pilot candidates though program participants continued to attended classes at civilian colleges and universities (with flight training conducted by private flight schools).

At its peak, 1,132 educational institutions and 1,460 flight schools were participating in the pilot training program. The WTS program was phased out in the summer of 1944 but not before admirably achieving its primary mission "To fill the skies with pilots."

*(The U.S. Army Air Corps (USAAC) was established as the Army's air arm on July 2, 1926. To give the air arm a greater degree of operational and organizational freedom, it was reorganized as the U.S. Army Air Forces (USAAF) on June 20, 1941. However, the term "Air Corps" continued to be used by the general public—USAAF was the more inclusive designation. It was not until the establishment of the Department of Defense in 1947 that the U.S. Air Force (USAF) became a separate service, joining its sister services—the U.S. Navy, U.S. Marine Corps, and U.S. Army—on September 18 , 1947.)

Above: Dr. Frederick D. Patterson, president of Tuskegee Institute, and George L. Washington, general manager, Division of Aeronautics, Tuskegee Institute. Below: The CAA pilot's license of Chief Pilot Charles Alfred Anderson of Bridgeport, Pennsylvania.

Flight instructor briefs aviation cadets on the day's training assignments.

Chief Pilot Charles Anderson, second from right, briefs a cadet before his solo flight in a PT-17, the primary trainer at Tuskegee. George L. Washington, general manager, in civilian clothing, stands at far right.

Instructors catch up on the local newspapers during a break in flying training operations. Chief Pilot Charles Anderson is in the center.

From left, General Manager George L. Washington, President Frederick Patterson, and Chief Pilot Charles Anderson, the Institute's first flight instructor, admire Tuskegee's first plane, a Waco UPF-7, July 29, 1940.

Above: Key administrative personnel in the Division of Aeronautics. The general manager was responsible directly to the president of Tuskegee Institute for efficient operation of Tuskegee Institute's Pilot Training School. Assembled are supervisors and heads of flying, ground school, aircraft maintenance, physical plant, and business departments for both Kennedy Field ("Airport Number One") and Moton Field.

Below: Division of Aeronautics instructors stationed at "Airport Number One." Notice CPT insignia on their hats.

Above: A group of aviation cadets on the flight line at Kennedy Field, Tuskegee.

Right: Lewis A. Jackson, director of Civilian Pilot Training. Note the unique hat brass. Jackson went on to have a distinguished career as an educator at Central State University in Wilberforce, Ohio, from which he retired as president. A lifelong entrepreneur, he faithfully worked on designing a "roadable" airplane that could be stored at home and towed or driven to the airport.

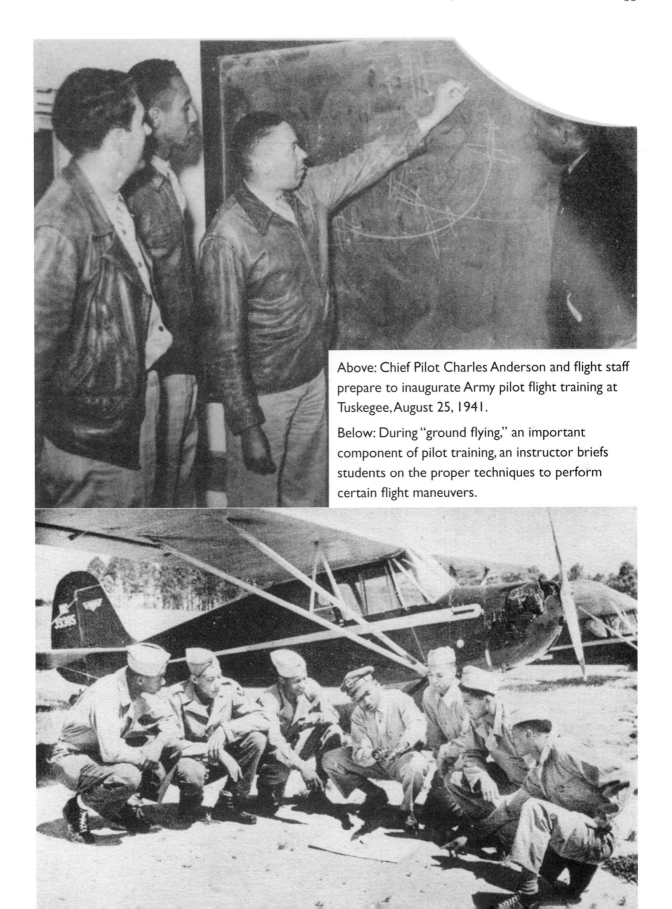

Above: Chief Pilot Charles Anderson and flight staff prepare to inaugurate Army pilot flight training at Tuskegee, August 25, 1941.

Below: During "ground flying," an important component of pilot training, an instructor briefs students on the proper techniques to perform certain flight maneuvers.

Early morning scene on the flight line at "Airport Number One." These JP-3 Piper light planes were used for aviation cadet candidates' Indoctrination Flight Training.

Each instructor "pre-flights" his students as a first step in the course. Here he is shown demonstrating the proper method of "swinging the prop" of a JP-3 Piper.

Above: Chief Pilot Anderson gives a formation of entering trainees a preview of the training and objectives of the Indoctrination Flight Course.

Below: The Assistant Chief of Maintenance gives a detailed lecture-demonstration to entering trainees regarding the aircraft and engine. After being taught how to accomplish the daily inspection, the trainee himself conducted the inspection under supervision.

Early in their training, students at Tuskegee flew JP-3 Piper light planes while completing the Indoctrination Flight Course.

Handling paperwork in the program's administrative offices.

In March 1941, First Lady Eleanor Roosevelt visited the Civilian Pilot Training Program, "Airport Number One" (Kennedy Field), Tuskegee. G. L. Washington, program director, introduces Mildred Hemmons, a student pilot, while Dr. F. D. Patterson, president of Tuskegee Institute looks on. Hemmons had received her private pilot's license in February 1941. In the background are CPT students Quinton Gaillard and Daniel "Chappie" James (in "T" letter sweater), James entered the U.S. Army Air Forces in 1943, and in 1975 he became the first black four-star Air Force general.

During her visit Mrs. Roosevelt requested an orientation flight. Chief Pilot Charles Anderson flew the First Lady over the area in one of the field's training aircraft.

Left: Aviation Cadet Alexander Anderson poses with his future wife, Hattye Grimmett. At the time of this photo, she had recently been crowned "Miss Tuskegee Institute."

Right: Anderson beams with pride following his graduation from Tuskegee Institute's first Civilian Pilot Training Program class. Anderson had written NAACP Executive Director Walter White three times in 1941 expressing his desire to serve in the Air Corps on a segregated or integrated basis. Subsequently admitted to the CPT program, he had the second highest score on the Civilian Aviation Authority's ground school exam. Though considered to be a highly proficient pilot, his white Advanced Pilot Training School instructor refused to solo him (he later soloed for George "Spanky" Roberts). Anderson went on to become a liaison pilot during World War II and later served in Korea and Vietnam. He was also a helicopter pilot and one of the first black command sergeant majors in the U.S. Army.

Dr. William H. Hastie
Civilian Aide to the
Secretary of War
Washington, D.C.

8814 Blaine Avenue
Cleveland, Ohio
December 21, 1942

Dear Dr. Hastie:

I am writing this letter to inform you of an instance of discrimination that I encountered recently at the hands of the U.S. Army Air Corps. Before citing the case I shall give you a brief background.

Since June, 1941, I have been a student in aviation courses given by the Civil Aeronautics Administration designed to furnish pilots for the armed services. Upon completion of my course in November, 1942, I received a letter from the Army Air Corps base at Maxwell Field, Alabama, asking me to report there on or about Dec., 1, 1942, to take further training in the Army Instructor School maintained at that field.

When I reported to this field, I was not permitted to enter the school solely because I was a Negro. The man to whom I talked at Maxwell Field (Mr. Feest, Room 125, Austin Hall) told me that Negroes were not trained there.

I am sending this brief outline of the situation in order that you may take appropriate measures to correct this injustice or in order that you may tell me what I should do to achieve the same result.

Yours sincerely,

Gilbert A. Cargill

This letter (typed for clarity) from aviation student Gilbert Cargill to the War Department demonstrates the discrimination African Americans faced in trying to become military pilots prior to creation of the Tuskegee Airmen. Maxwell Field (today Maxwell AFB) was only forty miles from Tuskegee.

This restored PT-17 airplane is on display at the Tuskegee Airmen National Historic Site at Moton Field, Tuskegee, Alabama.

2

Primary Flying Training

In late 1938, an Army Air Corps board of officers recommended contracting with civilian schools to provide primary pilot training for 4,500 trainees over a two-year period. Under the contract, the government provided the schools with training aircraft, flying clothes, textbooks and equipment. The schools were to furnish the instructors, training sites, facilities, aircraft maintenance, quarters, and mess halls. Initially, nine civilian schools began primary pilot training under this arrangement during the winter of 1938–39. Others schools would be added later, among them Tuskegee Institute, located in Tuskegee, Alabama.

The War Department approved Tuskegee's contract on June 7, 1941. The resulting primary training program was identical to the ones offered at other colleges and universities. The program consisted of sixty-five flying hours that were spread out over a ten-week period and covered the four areas of pre-solo, intermediate, accuracy, and acrobatic flying. Though the program called for ten aviation cadets to enter the initial course, the first class, designated as Class 42-C (the "C" referred to the month; there were no "A" or "B" classes in 1942), began pilot training at Tuskegee with thirteen students. With construction at Tuskegee's primary flying training installation delayed because of heavy rains, training began at nearby Kennedy Field on August 21. Two days later, the program moved to its permanent home at Moton Field.

Unfortunately, only six of the original thirteen cadets completed the course. They would move on to nearby Tuskegee Army Air Field to begin basic flying training. These courageous young men had completed the first step in a long journey toward racial equality and toward fulfilling black America's dream of "filling the skies with black wings." By the end of World War II, approximately 250,000 students had graduated from 64 civilian primary pilot training contract schools located across the United States.

In August 1941, Major General Walter R. Weaver delivered the inaugural address initiating the training of African American cadets as military aviators for the United States Army Air Forces. Tuskegee Institute's Booker T. Washington Monument is in the background.

Above: A flight of aviation cadets marches toward the post flag pole in preparation for a retreat ceremony, June 1942. The daily retreat ceremony was one of the most inspiring ceremonies held on an Army post. Army Air Forces Training Command provided each aviation cadet with training in military drill and ceremonies, as well as technical and flying training.

Below: Nothing tops mail call and a letter from home.

Left: Stearman PT-17s at Moton Field.

Below: A group of aviation cadets stands in front of a PT -17, the primary trainer at Tuskegee. The cadet in the center is holding one of the mascots of the cadet corps.

Left: A class of aviation cadets at Tuskegee Army Air Field. Tuskegee Institute's Chief Pilot Charles A. Anderson is in the center of the front row.

Below: Another class of aviation cadets shown in front of the PT-17 primary trainer aircraft, April 1944.

Above: Mess hall line-up—happy faces and hungry stomachs.

Right: A corner of the mess hall at Tuskegee.

Above and Left: Relaxing on the Tuskegee Institute campus on a "no flying Sunday." Below: Daily retreat and flag-lowering ceremony. The cadet barracks is in the background.

Right: Aviation cadets at Tuskegee Army Air Field, study a radial aircraft engine during one of their ground school courses in June 1942.

Below: Field Day athletic competition. Every aviation cadet was expected to be physically fit and have a competitive spirit.

Left: A check pilot at Moton Field shows his family about on Field Day.

Below: Some of the clerical workers "dig out" from behind desks to witness aerial competition on Field Day.

Above: A cadet winner in Field Day aerial competition is rewarded with a ride in a Basic Flight Training plane, the aircraft he will fly after he completes Primary Flight Training.

Right: "Post-flight" critique.

3

BASIC FLYING TRAINING

After primary flight training in PT-17 airplanes at Tuskegee Institute's Moton Field, pilots transferred to Tuskegee Army Air Field, a military airfield belonging to the Army Air Forces, for the next phases of flying training before entering combat: basic, advanced, and transition pilot training.

Tuskegee Army Air Field, new like Moton, covered a much larger area, and included four runways. It lay a few miles to the northwest of Moton Field. Basic pilot training consisted of both ground school and flying training in military aircraft. Ground school courses included meteorology, radio communication, radio code, airplanes, engines, and navigation. The flying training took place in BT-13 airplanes, which, unlike the biplanes of Moton Field, had only one set of wings. The first advanced class began at Tuskegee Army Air Field on November 8, 1941.

The first group of cadets to enter the Basic and Advanced Flying School at Tuskegee Army Air Field. Only five successfully completed the flying training program and graduated on March 7, 1942.

At Tuskegee Field these four aircraft were the preferred trainers during the war: top to bottom, the PT-17, primary; the BT-13, basic; the AT-6, advanced; and the P-40, transition.

Nurses from the base hospital at Tuskegee Army Air Field receive familiarization training on one of the training aircraft. This training included an orientation ride in the BT-13 aircraft.

Above and Below: Base Commander Major James Ellison returns salute as he passes cadets during a review at Tuskegee Army Air Field. The cadets are wearing their winter flight uniforms.

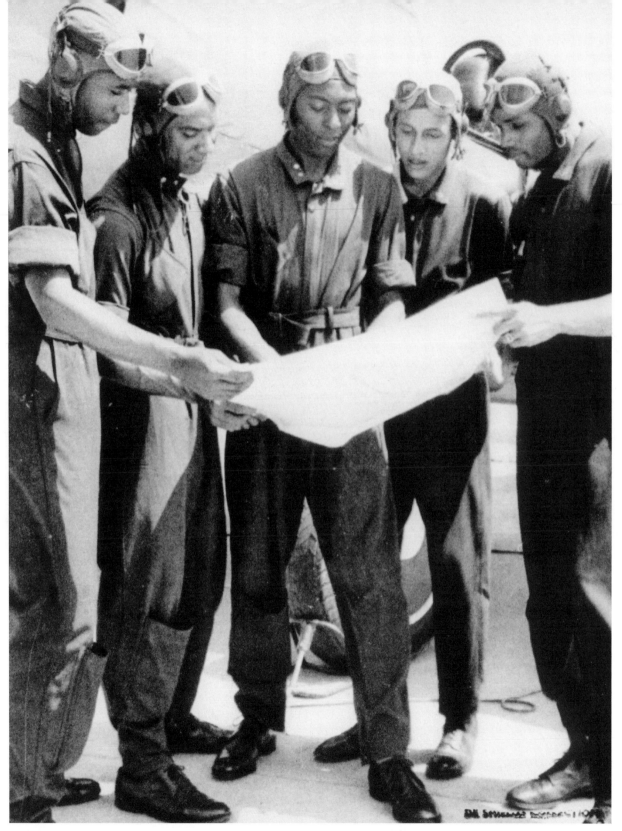

Cadets Haywood, Mosley, Robinson, and Faulkner review an aeronautical chart with instructor pilot before a flight from Tuskegee Army Air Field, 1943.

Above: Three aviation cadets report to their instructor in front of a line of Vultee BT-13 basic trainers. The instructor would take each cadet up for individual flying instruction. The cadets are wearing the flight uniform of the day.

Above: An instructor pilot points out the route and training areas on an aeronautical chart while he discusses the day's mission with three aviation cadets.

Right: Cadets received navigation training among the many subjects designed to prepare them as Army pilots. Here the cadets plot dead reckoning tracks during their hands-on training

Right: Captain Roy F. Morse, Army Air Forces, teaching aviation cadets how to send and receive code, Tuskegee Army Air Field, January 1942.

Below: Morse, center; on the left, from front to rear are James B. Knighten, Lee Rayford, and C. H. Flowers Jr.; on the right from front to rear are George Levi Knox, Sherman W. White, and Mac Ross.

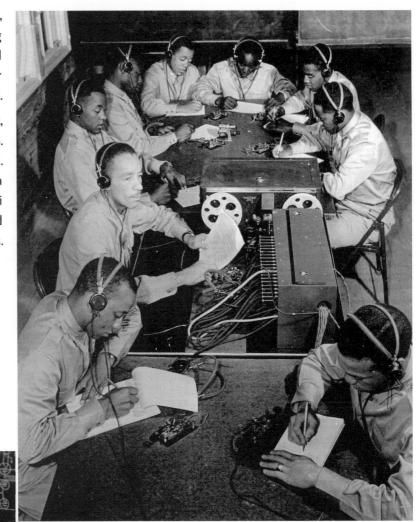

Above: Cadets doing their exercises in physical training at Tuskegee Army Air Field, June 1942.

Below: An aviation cadet at Tuskegee Army Air Field shown on his bunk in his barracks "studying" as he gazes fondly at his collection of photos of his girl friends.

Aviation cadets, instructors, and enlisted men from the 99th Pursuit Squadron attend a Commander's Call at Tuskegee Army Air Field, 1942.

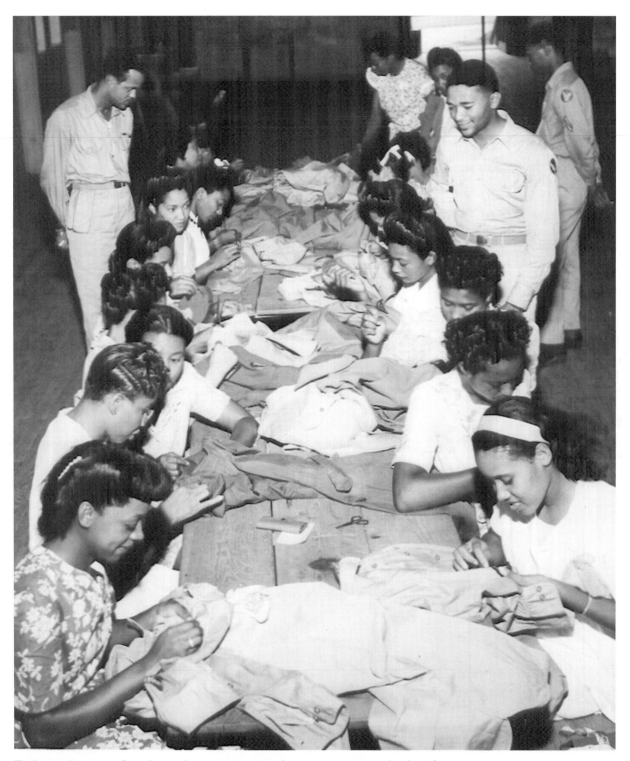

Tuskegee Institute female students sewing patches on aviation cadets' uniforms.

Above: Aviation cadets discuss the day's mission with their instructor during basic pilot training at Tuskegee Army Air Field, June 1942.

Right: Tuskegee cadets in armament class study the .30-caliber machine gun, June 1942.

Basic and Advanced Flying School for African American aviation cadets at Tuskegee Army Air Field. Lieutenant Donald B. McPherson, director of Tuskegee Basic Training, explains a cross-county flight using an aviation chart as cadets look on. Left to right: Lemuel R. Custis, Mac Ross, Charles DeBow, Frederick W. Moore, C. H. Flowers Jr., George Levi Knox, Lt. Donald B. McPherson, Lee Rayford, Sherman W. White, George S. "Spanky" Roberts, and James B. Knighten.

Right: Barracks inspection at Tuskegee Army Air Field.

Below: A typical cadet locker ready for inspection.

Right: Pay day in the Barracks at the Pilot Training School, Tuskegee Institute.

Cadets sitting at attention before a meal in the mess hall.

Secretary of War Henry L. Stimson was skeptical about proposals for training blacks as pilots. Nevertheless, Stimson (with cane) subsequently visited Tuskegee Field where he was greeted by Lieutenant General Barton K. Yount (center), commander of the Army Air Forces Training Command. Although the photograph includes Benjamin O. Davis Jr., Stimson did not actually meet Davis during his visit. To satisfy a request from military headquarters in Washington, Army Air Forces officials had a photograph of Davis superimposed on the photograph of Stimson's arrival, thus giving the impression that Davis had met the secretary while he was at Tuskegee. The incident is related in Davis's autobiography *American: An Autobiography* (Washington: Smithsonian Institution Press, 1991).

Above: Cadets at the Basic and Advanced Flying Training School participated in a wide variety of athletic events, such as this intramural baseball game.

Left: Rochester and Leon Rene entertain aviation cadets and staff during a United Service Organization (USO) performance, Tuskegee Army Air Field, January 1942.

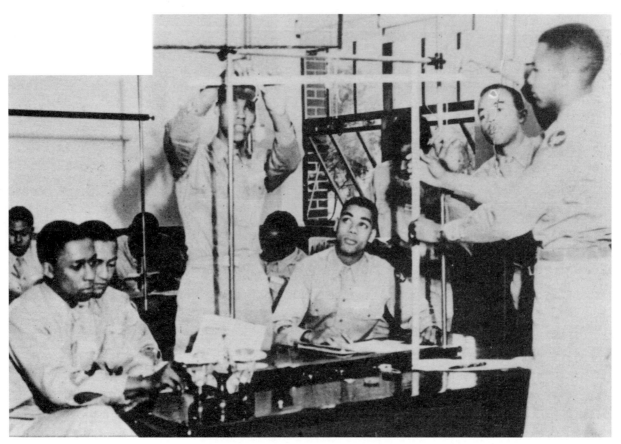

Above: Aviation cadet candidates of the 2211th Air Base Unit (College Training, Aircrew) received their major academic course training on the Tuskegee Institute campus. The photography above shows a physics class.

Above: Captain Benjamin Oliver Davis Jr., of Washington, D.C., climbing into an Advanced Trainer at Tuskegee Army Air Field in January 1942.

Right: Howard A. Wooten received his pilot wings when he graduated December 1944 from the Army Air Forces Basic and Advanced Flying School, Tuskegee.

U.S. Army Air Forces Colonel Noel F. Parrish assumed command of the Tuskegee Army Air Field on December 26, 1942. Parrish, a native of Lexington, Kentucky, was born on November 11, 1909. In 1928, he graduated from Rice Institute, Houston, Texas. After a year of graduate study, he entered the Army as a private on July 30, 1930 and a year later became a flying cadet in the first basic class to be trained at the newly constructed Randolph Field, San Antonio, Texas. In July 1932, he completed advanced training at Kelly Field, also in San Antonio. He was sent to Tuskegee Institute to command the newly activated 66th Army Air Force Training Detachment in May 1941. He and the first class of cadets to complete primary training were transferred to the Advanced Flying School at the new Tuskegee Army Air Field where he became director of training and later commander.

On March 7, 1942, the first Tuskegee Airmen graduated from Advanced Flying Training and were commissioned as second lieutenants. The graduates are shown here on a BT-13 basic training aircraft. From left: Charles DeBow Jr., a business administration graduate of Hampton Institute; Lemuel R. Custis, a policeman from Hartford, Connecticut, Mac Ross, a Howard University graduate who had been an inspector at an Ohio iron works; Captain Benjamin O. Davis Jr., (seated in the aircraft), the first black graduate from West Point in the twentieth century and the man who would later command the 99th Pursuit Squadron overseas; George S. "Spanky" Roberts, a graduate of West Virginia State College; and Lieutenant R. M. Long, their instructor pilot.

TUSKEGEE AIRMEN LOCATIONS IN THE UNITED STATES

1   Alabama: Tuskegee (Tuskegee Institute, Moton Field, Kennedy Field, and Tuskegee Army Air Field); Montgomery (Montgomery Airport/Gunter Field) and Maxwell Air Force Base)

2   Ohio: Lockbourne Army Air Base

3   Michigan: Selfridge Field; Oscoda Army Air Field

4   Illinois: Chanute Air Force Base

5   Kentucky: Godman Field

6   Indiana: Freeman Field

7   South Carolina: Walterboro Army Air Field

8   Florida: Eglin Army Air Field

9   Mississippi: Keesler Field

10   Texas: Hondo Army Air Field; Midland Army Air Field

11   New York: Buffalo: Curtis Technical Training School

12   New Jersey: Camp Kilmer

4

ADVANCED FLYING TRAINING

After pilots completed basic flying training at Tuskegee Army Air Field, using BT-13 monoplanes, they were ready for the next stage of their instruction, which was advanced flying training.

The first advanced flying training class at Tuskegee began in January 1942. For the flying training, the pilots flew AT-6 aircraft, which did not appear very different from the BT-13s, but were more advanced and maneuverable, like the fighters most of the graduates would eventually fly. Ground courses consisted of armament, gunnery, tactics and techniques of air fighting, advanced navigation, maintenance, and engineering. For the gunnery and combat tactics, the pilots in the advanced training stage used ranges at Eglin Field, Florida.

The advanced flight training was followed at Tuskegee Army Air Field, unlike most other basic and advanced flying training bases, by transition training. Single-engine pilots learned how to fly P-40 aircraft, which were of the same type as fighters flown in combat theaters. The 99th Fighter Squadron flew P-40s when it first entered combat in North Africa and later in Italy.

Twin-engine pilots learned instead how to fly AT-10s, which prepared them to fly medium bombers such as the B-25, which also had two engines. Some of the A-10 pilot graduates from Tuskegee Army Air Field moved on to Mather Field, California, where they learned how to fly the B-25 aircraft types used later by the 477th Bombardment Group. By March 1945, Tuskegee Army Air Field had a training version of the B-25 of its own, to replace the AT-10.

Above: Cadets reporting to Captain Benjamin O. Davis Jr., commandant of cadets, Tuskegee, September 1941.

Tent camp at the Advanced Flying School, Tuskegee Field, in fall 1941 and spring 1942 before all of the barracks were completed. Each squad tent housed six to eight cadets or enlisted men, .

Top: Colonel Noel F. Parrish, commanding officer of Tuskegee Army Air Field (front row, fourth from the left) with his base staff and instructor pilot cadre pose for an official photograph in 1943.

Bottom: The newly constructed Post Headquarters at the Advanced Flying School, Tuskegee Army Air Field, in November 1941.

A student in Advanced Pilot Training gets a critique from his instructor on a just-completed solo mission.

Top: Aviation cadets at the Advanced Flying School, Tuskegee Army Air Field, prepare for a retreat formation, September 1, 1942.

Center: Major General Benjamin O. Davis Sr. visited the Advanced Flying School, Tuskegee Army Air Field, November 2, 1943. Shown with the general are Colonel Noel F. Parrish, commanding officer, Tuskegee AAF, and Lieutenant Colonel Benjamin O. Davis Jr., soon to become the commanding officer of the 99th Pursuit Squadron.

Bottom: Base Operations and training buildings, Tuskegee Army Air Field, November 1943.

Shooting skeet, hanging out with friends in the barracks reception room, and writing letters home were among the many activities available to the aviation cadets during off-duty hours.

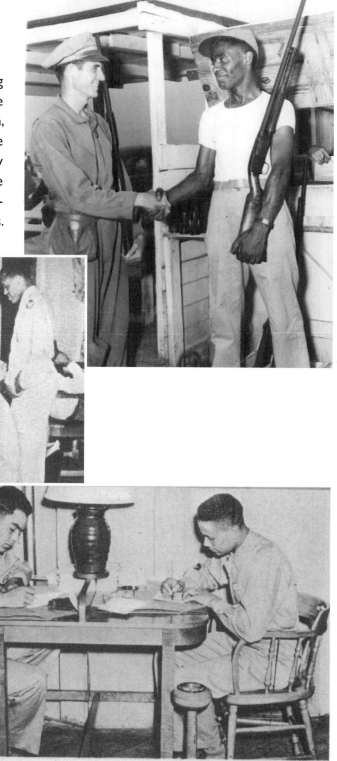

Left: As part of his comprehensive flying training course, an aviation cadet practices instrument flying in a Link Trainer at Tuskegee Army Air Field, June 1942.

Below: Aviation cadets and ground crew personnel stand by their AT-6 advanced training aircraft at Tuskegee Army Air Field. In that nine-week phase of training, the cadets received seventy flying hours in either the AT-6 or the P-40 trainers

Left: Colonel Noel F. Parrish, commanding officer of Tuskegee Army Air Field, stands with six freshly commissioned second lieutenants, while a Tuskegee Institute official observes.

Center: Aviation cadets at their group review, or graduation parade.

Bottom: The Tuskegee Army Air Field Band plays for the occasion.

5

Training Beyond Tuskegee

Primary, basic, advanced, and transition training for pilots at Tuskegee Army Air Field was just the beginning for the black pilots who trained there. Although the 99th Fighter Squadron deployed directly from Tuskegee to overseas duty in North Africa in April 1943, the three other fighter squadrons at Tuskegee, along with the 332nd Fighter Group to which they belonged, moved to Selfridge Field in Michigan for further training. The group and its 100th, 301st, and 302nd fighter squadrons remained at Selfridge from the end of March 1943 to early April 1943, when they moved to Oscoda, also in Michigan. In early July, the group and its squadrons moved back to Selfridge where they remained until the end of the year. During its time at Selfridge and Oscoda, the 332nd Fighter Group honed its skills with fighters designed in part to strike ground targets on tactical missions, including P-40s like the ones with which it trained at Tuskegee, and P-39s that it would use after deployment overseas.

After the 332nd Fighter Group and its three squadrons deployed from Selfridge at the end of 1943, the first and only African American bombardment group was activated at Selfridge, in January 1944. The training of a bombardment group took longer than a fighter group, partly because it included not only pilots but also crewmen such as navigators and bombardiers. While the bomber pilots trained in B-25s at Selfridge, the bombardiers and navigators trained at other bases. The 477th Bombardment Group moved in May 1944 to Godman Field, Kentucky, not merely because it was in the South, which was more racially segregated, but also because the climate was better there for flying, particularly in the winter.

The 477th Bombardment Group moved again in early March 1945, as the weather warmed up, from Godman Field to Freeman Field, Indiana, a larger base that seemed to be an improvement over Godman. However, the new base was a blessing and a curse. The larger field allowed the commander to designate two different buildings as officers' clubs, claiming one would be for training officers and one for trainees. The real purpose was racial segregation, which violated the current Army Air Forces regulations. African American officers at Freeman Field refused to be segregated, resulting in the "Freeman Field Mutiny" [see page 22]. To resolve the racial problems, the Army Air Forces replaced the 477th Bombardment Group's white commander with Colonel Benjamin O. Davis Jr., who had commanded the 332nd Fighter Group in successful combat in Europe. The 99th Fighter Squadron was also reassigned from the 332nd Fighter Group to the 477th Bombardment Group, and the group was redesignated as the 477th Composite Group, because it then had both bombers and fighters. The 332nd Fighter Group in the meantime was inactivated, leaving the 477th at that time as the only black group in the Army Air Forces.

With black leadership, the 477th Composite Group continued to prepare for combat overseas, but the chance never came. Faced with atomic attacks and a Soviet declaration of war, the Japanese surrendered before the black pilots of the 477th could use their bombers and fighters against them.

Behind the Tuskegee Airmen pilots were many others who could also call themselves Tuskegee Airmen but who never got to fly an airplane. Many were other officers, such as the navigators and bombardiers who flew as air crew members on the B-25s. Many of them trained at bases beyond those where the pilots trained. For example, Tuskegee Airmen navigators trained at the Army Air Forces Navigation School at Hondo Army Air Field in Texas. Behind every Tuskegee Airman officer were many enlisted men who supported them and without whom they would not have succeeded. They included maintenance personnel, ordnance personnel, quartermasters, guards, engineers, supply personnel, and other specialists. Among the bases where enlisted personnel in the Tuskegee Airmen organizations trained were Chanute Field, Illinois (where the 99th Fighter Squadron was first activated); Keesler Field, Mississippi; Midland Field, Texas; Fort Monmouth, New Jersey; the Curtis-Wright Factory Training School in Buffalo, New York; and cities and towns that included Atlanta, Georgia; Lincoln, Nebraska; Indianapolis, Indiana; Tomah, Wisconsin. In fact, personnel who served as Tuskegee Airmen trained and served at bases all over the United States and in a host of units beyond the squadrons of the 332nd Fighter Group and the 477th Bombardment Group.

Aircraft safety depended on the efficiency of ground crew checks, inspections, and maintenance, as well as preflights before every flight.

Above: Tuskegee Institute President Frederick D. Patterson and Tuskegee Division of Aeronautics Director George L. Washington inspect training of the 99th Pursuit Squadron ground crew at Chanute Field, Illinois, summer of 1941.

Below: Patterson and Washington visited armament, engineering, and communications trainees at Chanute Field. From left: William R. Thompson, Nelson S. Brooks, Elmer D. Jones, James L. Johnson, Washington, Dudley W. Stevenson, Patterson, and William D. Townes.

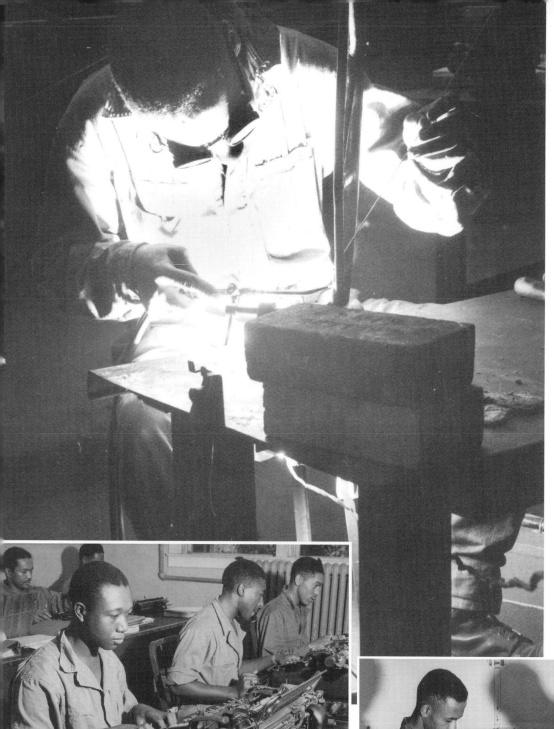

Personnel of the 99th Pursuit Squadron undergoing welding (Left), armament (Below Right), and teletype operator/maintenance (Below Left) training at Chanute Field, 1941.

99th Pursuit Squadron, Chanute Field, 1941: Four aircraft mechanic students (Top) inspect the main landing gear on a medium bomber during a class exercise. A field exercise provided valuable instruction in radio communications for these 99th Pursuit Squadron students (Left) from Chanute Field, Illinois.

Right : 99th Pursuit Squadron, Chanute Field, 1941. Students receive hands-on technical training in radial engine maintenance. Their Aircraft Engine Mechanics classroom contained of engines mounted for easy student and instructor access.

Above: Private William Cobb leads members of the 99th Pursuit Squadron Glee Club in a song at Chanute Field, 1941.

Below: 99th Pursuit Squadron technical training students pause for a meal in their squadron mess hall, Chanute Field, 1941.

Top: 99th Pursuit Squadron technical training graduating class at Chanute Field. From left, C. Howard, O. Handy, W. Lane, S. Cooke, R. Henderson, H. Benson, T. Combes, M. Edwards, C. Feaster, H. Thorton, W. Watson, J. White, I. Smedley; back row: A. Searcy, A. Harris; I. Smith, P. Moss, I. Cliff, W. Byrd, L. Beard, I. Howard, J. Freeman, R. Eaton, H. Jones, W. Griffin, P. Freeman, and E. Facen.

Bottom: Graduating class of 99th Pursuit Squadron aircraft mechanics in front of a hangar at Chanute Field.

Tuskegee Airmen in one of the flight formations which would soon carry them over enemy territory. Here they are flying the shark-nosed P-40 fighter aircraft on a 1943 practice mission from Selfridge Field, Michigan.

Left: Nelson Brooks of the 99th Pursuit Squadron undergoing radio maintenance training at Chanute Field, 1941.

Below: Tuskegee Airmen aircraft engine mechanic students get hands-on training disassembling cylinder heads at Keesler Field, Mississippi, 1943.

Left: Building T-662 at Chanute Field, June 1943. At that time the black students from the 99th Pursuit Squadron were kept segregated from other students receiving training and this building served as their recreation center.

Below: Five 99th Pursuit Squadron instructors from the Chanute Field staff that provided technical training in armament, engineering, communications, and aircraft maintenance.

A B-25 waist gunner handles the .50-caliber machine gun. This Tuskegee Airman was appropriately dressed for the extreme temperatures at high altitudes.

Right: Tuskegee Airmen pilots at Selfridge Field being briefed for a practice bombing mission as if they were under actual combat conditions3.

Below: Members of the first Tuskegee Airmen navigation cadet class received their commissions in the Army Air Forces on February 16, 1944. The class visited New York's City Hall as the guests of Mayor Fiorello H. La Guardia, shown here shaking hands with commanding officer Major Galen B. Price.

Boxers Jackie Wilson (left) and Ray Robinson fought each other in the ring, but at New York's Mitchel Field, they were Sergeant Wilson and Private Robinson in the same aviation squadron.

Above: Lena Horne
with Tuskegee Airmen
enlisted men, 1945.

Right: Bill "Bojangles"
Robinson entertains
troops at Godman
Field, Kentucky.

Aviation Cadet Alexander Anderson (front seat) and Staff Sergeant V. P. Cook prepare for a liaison pilot training flight. Liaison pilots—World War II aviators whose wings bore an "L" in the center—included many enlisted aviation students who had washed out of pilot training after having soloed. These pilots flew varied and often hazardous missions in nearly every theater. They flew medical evacuations from forward areas; delivered munitions, blood plasma, mail, and other supplies to the front lines; ferried personnel; flew photographic and intelligence missions; and served as air observers for fighters and bombers.

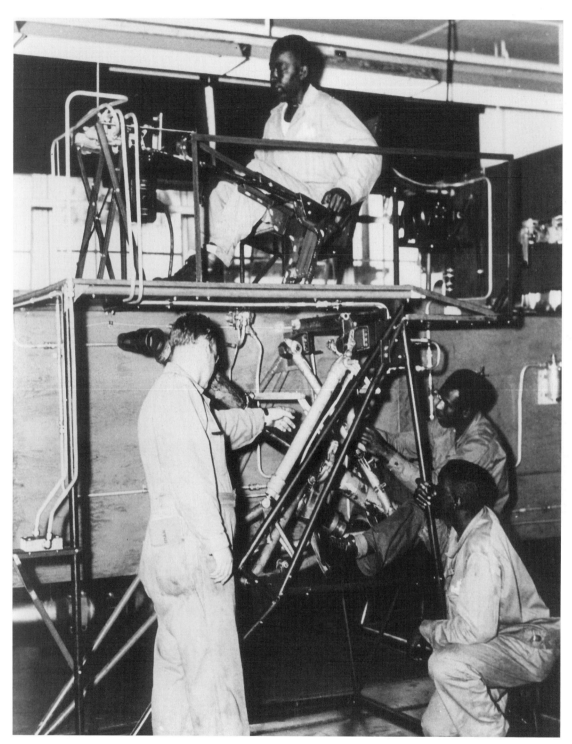

At Mississippi's Keesler Field, 1944, Tuskegee Airmen aircraft maintenance students worked with a hydraulics trainer.

Keesler Field graduated its first class of black airplane mechanics in August 1944. The men then rejoined their bombardment group at Selfridge Field.

SIGNIFICANT TUSKEGEE AIRMEN LOCATIONS OVERSEAS

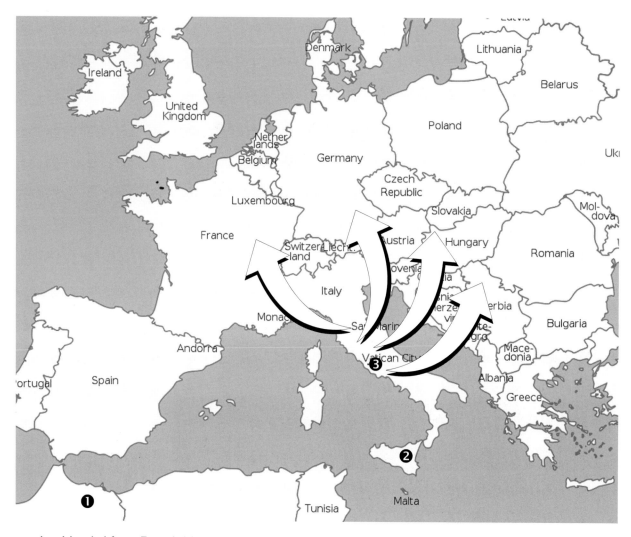

1   North Africa: French Morocco; Tunisia

2   Sicily: Licata; Termini; Barcellona

3   Italy: Foggia; Madna; Capodichino; Cercola; Pignataro; Ciampino; Orbetello; Ramitelli; Cattolica; Montecorvina; Lucera

Arrows indicate directions of typical long-range bomber escort missions the Tuskegee Airmen flew from their base at Ramitelli, Italy, into central and eastern Europe in support of the Fifteenth Air Force. Prior to moving to Ramitelli, the Tuskegee Airmen units had flown many tactical missions within Italy for the Twelfth Air Force.

Note: This map uses present-day country borders rather than those that existed during World War II.

Part 2

OVERSEAS DEPLOYMENT

North Africa

Sicily

Italy

Staff officers of the 99th Fighter Squadron near Fez, French Morocco, May 12, 1943. From left: Lieutenant Colonel Benjamin O. Davis, executive officer commanding; Captain Hayden C. Johnson, adjutant; Captain E. Jones, service detachment; Lieutenant William R. Thompson, armaments; Lieutenant Herbert E. Carter, engineers; Lieutenant Erwin B. Lawrence, operations; Lieutenant George R. Currie, ordnance.

6

TUSKEGEE AIRMEN
IN COMBAT OPERATIONS

Commanding more interest than any other aspect of the Tuskegee Airmen experience is their combat record. While flying missions from North Africa, Sicily, and the mainland of Italy, the Tuskegee-trained pilots demonstrated that they could fly fighters in combat, that they could fly any kind of fighter aircraft on any kind of fighter mission, and that they could do it as well as their non-black compatriots and enemies.

The 99th Fighter Squadron was the first American black flying unit and also the first such unit in combat. It deployed from Tuskegee to North Africa during April 1943. Flying P-40s fighters, the squadron at first flew patrol missions to protect Allied shipping in the Mediterranean. While attached to various white fighter groups, although not assigned directly to them, the 99th joined white P-40 squadrons in attacking enemy targets on the Italian Mediterranean islands of Pantelleria and Sicily. After moving to Sicily and then to the mainland of Italy, the 99th scored impressive numbers of aerial victories while protecting American ground forces at Anzio from enemy aircraft attacks. During its combat operations in Italy, before it joined the 332nd Fighter Group, the 99th Fighter Squadron earned two Distinguished Unit Citations.

In early 1944, the 332nd Fighter Group and its 100th, 301st, and 302nd Fighter Squadrons also deployed to Italy. Although the group at first flew P-39s in combat instead of P-40s, it conducted attacks on ground targets and flew patrol missions for the Twelfth Air Force, like the 99th, and occasionally escorted medium bombers raiding battlefield targets near the front.

By the summer of 1944, the mission of the Tuskegee Airmen changed dramatically, as the 332nd Fighter Group began escorting heavy bombers such as B-17s and B-24s on raids deep into enemy territory for the Fifteenth Air Force. Flying P-47s and later P-51 high-speed long-range fighters with tails painted red for group identification, the Tuskegee Airmen shot down increasing numbers of enemy fighters. Enemy aircraft shot down bombers the 332nd Fighter Group was assigned to protect on only seven of the 179 bomber-escort missions the group flew between early June 1944 and late April 1945. The total number of escorted bombers shot down was significantly less than the average number of bombers lost by the six other fighter escort groups of the Fifteenth Air Force. On the longest fighter-escort mission from Italy, on March 24, 1945, to Berlin, three Tuskegee Airmen each shot down a German jet that could fly significantly faster than their own red-tailed P-51 Mustangs. For this mission, the 332nd Fighter Group earned its only Distinguished Unit Citation. When the 332nd returned from Italy, it had proven that black fighter pilots were the equal of any others.

Left: Captain Erwin B. Lawrence, Cleveland, Ohio, assistant operations officer in the original 99th Fighter Squadron, sits in the cockpit following a bomber escort mission.

Below: Captain Andrew D. Turner signals to his ground crew before taking off from a base in Italy in September 1944. This Tuskegee Airman was a member of the 15th Air Force, which had been smashing enemy objectives in Germany and the Balkans with both fighters and bombers. The pilot's plane is a P-51 Mustang.

PILOT- Capt. A. D. Turner.
C/CHIEF- S/Sgt. A. Cochran.
Asst- Sgt. C. J. Bentley.
C/ARM- Cpl. H. Beguesse.

With Lieutenant Edward C. Gleed of Horton, Kansas, giving them pointers from a giant map, pilots of the P-51 Mustang 332nd Fighter Group learn their "target for today" during a September 1944 briefing at a base in Italy. Both the map and the briefing chart indicate that an objective in Germany will soon be on the receiving end of their bullets and bombs. These men are members of the Fifteenth Air Force, whose planes fly as part of the Mediterranean Allied Air Force.

Above: P-51 pilots, Italy, August 1944. From left, Lieutenants Dempsey W. Morgan Jr., Carroll S. Woods, and Robert H. Nelson Jr., Captain Andrew D. Turner, commanding officer of the 100th Fighter Squadron, and Lieutenant Clarence P. Lester, who had three enemy fighters to his credit.

Right: Sharing credit for Tuskegee Airmen victories were support personnel like mechanics George Johnson and James E. Howard, February 1944.

Above: Members of the original 99th Fighter Squadron pose in front of a P-40, which they used to escort medium bombers to the western sector of Sicily.

Below: Pilots of the 99th—credited with ten German planes shot down January 27, 1944, and three more the next day, over the new Allied beachheads south of Rome—photographed at a U.S. base in the Mediterranean Theater. These airmen, veterans of the North African and Sicilian campaigns, were formerly classmates at Tuskegee.

Above: Members of the 99th Fighter Squadron pose for a picture at the Anzio beachhead in February 1944. Capless in the foreground is Lieutenant Andrew Lane.

Right: Staff Sergeant Conige C. Mormon, a crew chief in the 332nd Fighter Group, cleans the glass of a pilot's P-51 Mustang piloted by Clarence D. Lester of Chicago.

At an awards ceremony in Italy, General Benjamin O. Davis Sr. pins the Distinguished Flying Cross on his son, Colonel Benjamin O. Davis Jr. of Washington, D.C. Waiting their turns to be decorated are Captain Joseph D. Elsberry of Langston, Oklahoma, and Lieutenants Jack D. Holsclaw of Spokane, Washington, and Clarence D. Lester, of Chicago.

2nd Lieutenant Edwin Johnson was a squadron photo officer.

Above: Six P-51 Mustangs of the 332nd Fighter Group buzz their home base in Italy after returning from a bomber escort mission. Below: Lieutenant Andrew D. Marshall, pilot in the 332nd Fighter Group of the Mediterranean Allied Air Force, had his plane shot up by flak during a strafing mission over Greece before the Allied invasion, October 1944. When he crash landed, about all that was left of his plane was the engine and himself. But he escaped with bruises and cuts. Greeks hid him from the Nazis, then directed him to British soldiers who had parachuted into Greece. Here Marshall tells an American pilot of the 51st Troop Carrier Wing of his harrowing experience.

Competition was intense among crew chiefs of the 332nd Fighter Group in Italy. Here Staff Sergeant William Accoo of Salem, N.H., washes his plane with soap and water. Next he will wax it. Note his reflection on the side of the P-51, September 1944.

Right: Captain Wendell O. Pruitt. a pilot of the Fifteenth Air Force, always made sure before a mission to leave his valuable ring with his crew chief, Staff Sergeant Samuel W. Jacobs, November 1944.

Left: Staff Sergeant Alfred D. Norris, crew chief in the 332nd Fighter Group, closes the canopy of a P-51 Mustang for his pilot. Captain William T. Mattison, operations officer of the Italy-based 100th Fighter Squadron.

Long, dangerous missions over enemy territory and during bad weather often saw fighter planes returning to their bases with minimal fuel remaining. Pilots of a Fifteenth Air Force squadron formed "the Three Minute Egg Club," with membership limited to those unfortunates who landed with less than a three-minute fuel reserve. From left, Lieutenants Clarence A. Dart, Wilson D. Eagleson, and William N. Olsbrook talk over their close calls.

Right: Tuskegee Airmen are among the servicemen scrambling for goods on the on the first day of operation of the post exchange store maintained by the 96th Air Service Group in Jesi, Italy. The store was managed by 1st Lt Byron Kuykendall of the 1051st Quartermaster Service Group (Aviation).

Below: In January 1945, the 1901st Quartermaster Truck Company of the 96th Air Service Group, was billeted in this castle at Jesi, Italy. Company histories note that the 96th ASG was "known up and down the peninsula as 'Weaver's Beavers'" and that "a duke once lived here."

Above: Heavyweight boxing champion Joe Louis was one of the most famous enlisted men in the U.S. Army during World War II. Staff Sergeant Louis regularly made morale tours like the one pictured here in 1944, when he refereed an intramural boxing match at a heavy-bomber base in Italy.

Left: Lieutenant Colonel Benjamin O. Davis Jr., commanding officer of the 99th Fighter Squadron, in his cockpit.

Two young Tuskegee Airmen take a break between flights.

Left: In the field, airmen work out the solution to a tough challenge.

Below: Private John T. Fields of the 332nd Fighter Group inspects the ammunition in a P-51 Mustang. Ground crews took all precautions to make sure their pilots' guns did not jam while on a mission.

Perhaps Captain Charles B. Hall of Brazil, Indiana, received more fame as a pilot than any black other than Colonel Benjamin O. Davis Jr. On July 2, 1943, Hall shot down a Focke-Wulf 190 over Castelvetrano, Sicily, becoming the first black in U.S. military service to destroy an enemy aircraft in aerial combat. He was personally congratulated by General Dwight D. Eisenhower, Allied Commander in Chief; Major General James H. Doolittle, Commanding Officer at the time of the North African Strategic Air Forces; Lieutenant General Carl Spaatz, then commander of the Twelfth Air Force; and British Air Vice Marshal Arthur Coningham, who was Commander in Chief of Northwest African Tactical Air Force. Hall later won the Distinguished Flying Cross for combat action in January 1944.

Ground crew members prepare to load bombs on P-40s of the 99th Fighter Squadron. The bombs were towed on specially built trailers from the bomb dump to the flight line.

Flight Officer James O. Bryson wearing the garrison hat (eagle on front) and the winter blouse with U.S. flying insignia on the lapel. The "fifty-mission crush" appearance of the hat was created by removing its grommet.

These airmen's attire belies their swagger. They look like flyers who have just been rescued.

Crew members of the 332nd Fighter Group receive their pre-mission briefing. The mission status board in visible in the background.

Four 332nd Fighter Group pilots head for their P-51s after the daily mission briefing. They will soon be on a bomber-escort mission over enemy territory.

Tuskegee Airman Herbert Carter stayed in the Air Force after World War II and rose to the rank of lieutenant colonel. Here he studies the recently completed "nose art" on the P-40 Warhawk he flew over Europe with the 99th Fighter Squadron. Most such aircraft art featured female names and imagery. The "Mike" on his plane probably mystified observers who did not know that it was the nickname of Carter's wife, Mildred, who incidentally was a pilot herself and a graduate of Tuskegee's Civilian Pilot Training program.

Fitted with a parachute harness and an inflatable life vest, this Tuskegee
Airman was ready for the worst.

Above: Home base for the 99th Fighter Squadron in Italy. From here the Tuskegee Airmen flew a variety of combat missions.

Below: Ground crewmen of an Italy-based 332nd Fighter Group Squadron place a loaded wing tank on a P-51 Mustang before the group takes off on another mission escorting bombers over enemy targets. The squadron used the auxiliary fuel tanks for long-distance flights. From left: Sergeants Charles K. Haynes, James A. Sheppard, and Frank Bradley.

Left: Tuskegee Airmen who were fighting overseas did not remain permanently in combat areas until the end of the war. Captains Lemuel R. Custis (left) and Charles B. Hall, of the 99th Fighter Squadron were photographed chatting together while they were on leave in New York City in June 1944.

Below: This photograph of 1st Lieutenant Lee Rayford was published with the notation that he had recently returned to the United States from Italy where he had served with the 99th Fighter Squadron. The article mentioned that other pilots formerly assigned to the 99th who were also back in America included 1st Lieutenants Walter I. Lawson, Charles W. Dryden, Graham Smith, and Luis R. Prunell.

Members of the 96th Air Service Group, stationed at Jesi, Italy, enjoy a dance and a break from war operations, January 1945.

The above scene at Jesi, Italy, shows a section of the motor pool of the 1901st QM Truck Company (Aviation) two days after a January 1945 snow storm. Note the castle on the horizon where personnel were quartered.

Above: Ambulance and driver at one of the Tuskegee Airmen bases.

Below: A contingent of bombardier-navigators with group navigator.

≋ *Part 3* ≋

EPILOGUE

After World War II

The Tuskegee Airmen in History

Chronology of the Tuskegee Airmen

Junior officers faced an uncertain future after the war.

AFTER WORLD WAR II

Following Germany's surrender, activities at Tuskegee Army Air Field began to wind down. Only twenty pilots earned their wings at the field in September 1945, and there were just nine graduates the following month. By that time, students were being allowed to drop out of the program at any phase of the training. As would be expected, the number of faculty and staff at the school shrank along with the decrease in the student population.

Class 46A was the last to graduate from the program. Discussions then began over the future of the installation. Tuskegee's white population remained ambivalent toward the post-war operation of the school. They favored the field's continuation as long as it was under the control of a white officer. After all, local white businesses had benefited handsomely from the revenue the black training program had generated. But whites demanded that if the installation was not to remain under white control, it should be closed immediately. As a result, the Army Air Forces decided to close the school in mid 1946.

The school's demise, however, was not accomplished without additional controversy. Tuskegee Institute President Dr. Frederick Patterson wanted to keep the airfield open and recommended to General George Marshall that the school be made a permanent flying field for black pilots. Patterson's efforts were met with strong opposition from the black press, which accused him of trying to "promote segregation at a profit to his institution." Most national black leaders were demanding full integration of the Army Air Forces and were determined to settle for nothing less.

Thus, after the last group of aviation cadets earned their wings at Tuskegee, black pilot training moved to Randolph Field, Texas, and Williams Air Force Base, Arizona.

For all practical purposes during the immediate post-war era, the military remained segregated until July 26, 1948. At that time, President Harry S. Truman signed Executive Order 9980, ending segregation in the armed services, and called for "the equality of treatment and opportunity for all persons in the armed services without regard to race."

Thus, when black pilots entered combat in 1950 during the Korean War, they did so in integrated units. Many of them had earned their wings at Tuskegee and had later fought with the 99th Fighter Squadron and the 332nd Fighter Group. In fact, an integrated B-26 crew flew the last combat mission of that war. By the end of the Korean fighting, the Air Force had become a leader in the integration campaign and served as a model for other services.

THE TUSKEGEE UNITS

In late April 1945, Tuskegee Airmen escorted reconnaissance planes over Prague, Czechoslovakia. It would be their last mission because on May 8, 1945, the German high command surrendered. Shortly thereafter, the Army Air Forces began demobilizing the 332nd. By October the group had returned to the United States and again was confronted with the racism and discrimination that they had left behind. Nonetheless, they returned proudly having shown the world that black men could fly, fight, and win.

After the war, Tuskegee Airmen were assigned to the newly activated 477th Composite Group of two bomber squadrons and one fighter squadron. Here the air crew gives a post-mission debrief for the maintenance crew of one of the group's B-25 Mitchel bombers

The 477th Composite Group moved, in March 1946, from Godman Field Kentucky, to Lockbourne Army Air Base in Ohio. On July 1, 1947, the 477th was deactivated, and the 332nd Fighter Group was reactivated in its stead, at Lockbourne. The 332nd Fighter Group replaced the 477th as the only African American group in the Army Air Forces. That same year, the Army Air Forces itself was replaced by the United States Air Force, and the 332nd became the only African American group in the new service, and remained so until the Air Force was desegregated.

The performance of the Tuskegee Airmen during the war had indeed been impressive. These airmen had flown more than 1,500 missions, downed 112 enemy aircraft in the air, and destroyed 150 more planes on the ground. They had also demolished a large number of enemy facilities and communication equipment. At the same time, they safely escorted numerous B-17s and B-24s on bombing missions deep into enemy territory. For their efforts during the war, Tuskegee Airmen were awarded 96 Distinguished Flying Crosses and more than 700 other awards.

During the post-war era, the Tuskegee Airmen would receive yet another award. On May 2, 1949, the Las Vegas Air Force Base hosted the first continental United States Air Force (USAF) fighter gunnery competition. Plans were for the fighter gunnery event to become an annual competition similar to the United States Navy's "Top Gun" competition. The 332nd Fighter Group was one of the units participating in the meet. Competing against four other teams and flying obsolete P-47 propeller aircraft, the 332nd team led from the beginning and won the conventional aircraft division.

AFTER WORLD WAR II ≋ 133

Left: Tuskegee Airmen from the 332nd Fighter Group were the overall winners (reciprocating engine type aircraft) in 1949, in the first USAF Gunnery Meet held at Las Vegas AFB, Nevada.

Below: Lieutenant General Elwood Quesada inspects military police of the 332nd Fighter Wing on the flight line at Lockbourne Army Air Base.

The Tuskegee Airmen pilot of this B-25 Mitchel bomber prepares to taxi out from the ramp at Lockbume AFB, Ohio, on a navigation and bombing training mission.

A B-25 Mitchel bomber ground crew manually rotates the aircraft's propellers to keep the engine oil from thickening prior to an early morning mission at Lockburne AFB.

After the end of hostilities, Tuskegee Airmen officers and enlisted men settled into a more routine existence. At Lockbourne AFB in Ohio, work centered around training and readiness. There were also family events, official ceremonies, and public activities.

Right: Colonel B. O. Davis Jr., commanding officer, of the 332nd Fighter Wing, welcomes a delegation from Wilberforce University during a base tour.

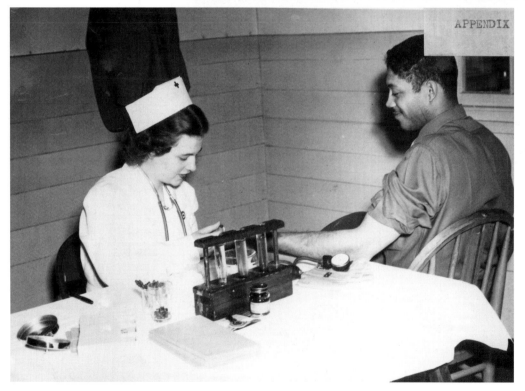

Above: American Red Cross worker Barbara Hedge prepares to take a donation from Staff Sergeant John Haynes of the 100th Fighter Squadron during a blood drive at Lockbourne AFB.

Dignitaries on the reviewing stand during Air Force Day at Lockbourne AFB. From left, Haley Bell, Governor Thomas J. Herbert, Mrs. B. O. Davis Jr., Mrs. Thomas J. Herbert, and Colonel B. O. Davis Jr. The boy plugging his ears is unidentified.

Routine administrative activity in the 332nd Fighter Wing Adjutant's office.

Left: 1st Lieutenant E. J. Williams is congratulated by Major Edward Gleed, wing executive officer, on receiving the Green Instrument Card. Williams was the base operations officer at the time.

Below: Children of base personnel receive Easter gifts from Daisy Crockett at an activity in the Lockbourne base gymnasium.

Top: Chaplain Alfred McWilliams officiates at wedding of Sergeant Willard Hardy and Francis Sharp, February 1948. The couple is flanked by attendants Charles Hardy and Cleona Belle.

Left: Corporal Charles H. Sorey of Bainbridge, Georgia, receives his high school diploma from 1st Lieutenant John J. Suggs, education and information officer, Lockbourne AFB, 1948.

Below: A Lockbourne civilian employee receives a cash prize from Wing Commander Colonel B. O. Davis Jr. for submitting a suggestion for a more efficient and less expensive method of cleaning aircraft spark plugs.

Church service being held beneath the wing of a bomber for the airmen performing maintenance on a Sunday, Godman Field, Kentucky.

Major Bases of the Tuskegee Airmen, 1941–1949

99th Fighter Squadron: Chanute Field, Illinois, March 22, 1941; Maxwell Field, Alabama, November 5 1941; Tuskegee, Alabama, November 10, 1941–April 2, 1943; Casablanca, French Morocco, April 24, 1943; Qued N'ja, French Morocco, April 29, 1943; Fardjouna, Tunisia, 7 June 1943; Licata, Sicily, 28 July 1943; Termini, Sicily, 4 September 1943; Barcellona, Sicily, 17 September 1943; Foggia, Italy, 17 October 1943; Madna, Italy, 22 November 1943; Capodichino, Italy, 16 Jan 1944; Cercola, Italy, 2 April 1944; Pignataro, Italy, 10 May 1944; Ciampino, Italy, 11 June 1944; Orbetello, Italy, 17 June 1944; Ramitelli, Italy, 6 July 1944; Cattolica, Italy, c. 5 May–June 1945; Godman Field, Kentucky, 22 June 1945; Lockbourne AAB (later, AFB), Ohio, 13 March 1946–1 July 1949.

332d Fighter Group: Tuskegee, Alabama, 13 October 1942; Selfridge Field, Michigan, 29 March 1943; Oscoda, Michigan, 12 April 1943; Selfridge Field, Michigan, 9 Jul-22 December 1943; Montecorvino, Italy, 8 February 1944; Capodichino, Italy, 15 April 1944; Ramitelli Airfield, Italy, 28 May 1944; Cattolica, Italy, c. 4 May 1945; Lucera, Italy, c. 18 July-September 1945; Camp Kilmer, New Jersey, 17-19 October 1945. Lockbourne AAB (later, AFB), Ohio, 1 July 1947-1 July 1949.

477th Bombardment Group (later, 477th Composite Group): Selfridge Field, Michigan, 15 Jan 1944; Godman Field, Kentucky, 6 May 1944; Freeman Field, Indiana, 5 March 1945; Godman Field, Kentucky, 26 April 1945; Lockbourne AAB, Ohio, 13 March 1946-1 July 1947.

8

THE TUSKEGEE AIRMEN IN HISTORY

The 332nd Fighter Group and its four squadrons proved that African Americans could fly the most advanced fighter aircraft in combat, and do it as well as anyone else. The 477th Bombardment Group and its four squadrons proved that black men could also fly multi-engined bombers at the head of air crews, and that they would not stand for segregated officers' clubs at the bases where they were stationed. Both groups, and the many other Tuskegee Airmen who did not fly aircraft but that also took part in the war in important ways, both at home and abroad, demonstrated that the decision to establish the Tuskegee program was a significant step in the direction of increasing opportunities for African Americans.

What became of the original Tuskegee Airmen? After World War II many left the Army Air Forces and became successful businessmen in the civilian world. Many also stayed in the new United States Air Force, and continued to demonstrate that African Americans could fulfill missions assigned to them, regardless of whether the duty had ever been assigned to them before. Benjamin O. Davis Jr., who had commanded both the 332nd Fighter Group and the 477th Composite Wing, remained in the service, and rose to become the first African American general in the United States Air Force. He eventually commanded the Thirteenth Air Force.

Daniel "Chappie" James, another Tuskegee Airman, also rose to become a general, and was named the first four-star African American general in the Air Force, after flying fighter missions during both the Korean and Vietnam wars. He eventually became commander of the North American Air Defense Command. Other Tuskegee Airmen also remained in the USAF and continued to serve with distinction, among them Colonels Clarence "Lucky" Lester and Charles McGee. The latter's mission total was among the highest of any military pilot.

Many other Tuskegee Airmen who continued to serve their country in the Air Force, and they inspired other African Americans to become pilots. Jesse L. Brown became the first black U.S. Navy pilot in 1949, and later Frank E. Peterson became the first black Marine Corps pilot to command a squadron in the Navy Department; he later rose to the rank of lieutenant general. Years later, Guion "Guy" Bluford became the first African American in space, taking part in the Space Shuttle program of the National Aeronautics and Space Administration. Lloyd "Fig" Newton became the first black Thunderbird pilot, and he later rose to become commander of the Air Education and Training Command, one of the most important commands in the Air Force.

Numerous other examples could be named. Suffice it to say that African Americans since World War II have continued to excel in the fields of aviation and space, not only as members of the Air Force, but also as members of other military services. They and countless others can thank the Tuskegee Airmen for helping to open the door of opportunity for them and for inspiring them to excel in a world still full of obstacles to overcome.

The Tuskegee Airmen, partly because of museum exhibits, newspaper and magazine articles, books, pamphlets, television documentaries, and even movies, have become part of the American cultural landscape, and the term "Tuskegee Airmen" has become familiar to most Americans since World War II.

The Tuskegee Airmen National Historic Site was established at Moton Field, and it was dedicated not long after the March 2007 ceremony in which President George W. Bush, on behalf of Congress, presented a collective gold medal to the Tuskegee Airmen. That medal is kept at the Smithsonian Institution in Washington, D.C., where the Smithsonian's National Air and Space Museum has a special "Black Wings" exhibit that includes the Tuskegee Airmen. The National Museum of the United States Air Force at Wright-Patterson Air Force Base also houses a Tuskegee Airmen exhibit, as does the National World War II Museum in New Orleans.

Countless other museums around the country celebrate the legendary "Red Tails" with audio and visual presentations. Even stretches of highways in some states are dedicated to the Tuskegee Airmen, including a stretch between Tuskegee and the state capital in Montgomery.

Lieutenant General Benjamin O. Davis Jr.

General Daniel "Chappie" James.

Tuskegee Airman "Chappie" James, shown above as a young officer in the 477th at Godman Field, and at left as a fighter pilot in Vietnam, rose to become the first four-star African American general in the U.S. Air Force.

Right: At a ceremony in 1998, President Bill Clinton pinned a fourth star on the shoulder of Benjamin O. Davis Jr., making him a full general in the U.S. Air Force. Davis's wife, Agatha, assisted Clinton with the pinning ceremony pictured above, and other Tuskegee Airmen veterans can be seen in the background. Clinton is wearing an honorary red jacket presented to him at the ceremony by the veterans. Davis had risen to become the first black general in the Air Force and had retired in 1970 as a three-star lieutenant general. A 1936 graduate of the U.S. Military Academy and the son of an Army general, Davis commanded the Tuskegee Airmen in combat during World War II. In 1970, after he retired from the Air Force, he was put in charge of the federal sky marshal program and later served as assistant secretary of the U.S. Department of Transportation. He and Mrs. Davis both died in 2002.

Left: The "Keep Us Flying. Buy War Bonds" poster (probably depicting Tuskegee Airman Lieutenant Robert W. Diez) was created in 1943 by an unidentified artist and was published to support the war effort. However, it has become an iconic image and is widely sold and displayed today, showing how the legend of the Airmen has entered popular culture.

Below: A poster depicting the life and career of Major Edward Gleed is another example of many works of art created to celebrate the legacy of the Tuskegee Airmen.

Above and facing page: Tuskegee Airmen veterans at the 1987 dedication of Roberts Hall at Chanute AFB.

Inset: George S. "Spanky" Roberts as a Tuskegee Airman 1st lieutenant.

Right: Then-Major Roberts, far right of photo, enjoying a light moment during World War II in the "Red Tails" war room at Ramitelli, Italy, with, from left, Truman Gibson, Colonel B. O. Davis Jr., Major General James M. Bevans, and Colonel Campbell.

Above: Tuskegee Airmen veterans were among the dignitaries in July 1987 at the posthumous dedication of Roberts Hall. the new visiting airmen quarters, at Chanute AFB. The hall is named for Tuskegee Airman Colonel George S. "Spanky" Roberts, the first black commander of the 99th Fighter Squadron and a former commander of the 332d Fighter Group.

Right: General Joel M. McKean, Chanute commander, and Mrs. Edith Roberts cut the ribbon during the dedication.

A banner welcoming the Tuskegee Airmen national convention and honoring the Airmen hangs in the in the Octave Chanute Aerospace Museum, Rantoul, Illinois. The banner commemorates the Tuskegee Airmen who trained at Chanute Field during World War II.

This mural, "The Black Eagles," graced the wall in one of the student dormitories at Chanute AFB.

Above: This mural by Roy LaGrone is titled "Col Noel F. Parrish, commanding officer, Tuskegee Army Flying School, and the first black pilots to receive wings in the Air Corps—1942." Depicted with Parrish are, from left, Lieutenants Mac Ross, Charles DeBow, and Lemuel R. Custis, Captain Benjamin O. Davis Jr., and Lieutenant George S. Roberts.

Left: The surviving Tuskegee Airmen are frequently invited today to military ceremonies such as the one depicted in this photo. General Alfred M. Gray, Marine Corps commandant, talks with Tuskegee Airmen George Walker III and Samuel Rhodes at the change-of-command ceremony in which Lieutenant General Frank E. Petersen retired.

Above: Tuskegee Airmen veterans take part in the dedication ceremony of the General Daniel "Chappie" James Center for Aerospace Science and Health Education at Tuskegee Airmen's Plaza, Tuskegee University. From left: From left: Henry Bowman, Chief Charles Alfred Anderson, Colonel Herbert Carter, Major Andrew Johnson.

Below: An F-4C Phantom II, the last aircraft flown in combat by James, is on display in front of the new center.

Several Tuskegee Airmen have been honored over the years by the Air Command and Staff College of Air University during the annual Gathering of Eagles meetings held at Maxwell Air Force Base.

Left: The 2007 Gathering honored Lieutenant Colonel Lee Archer, who shot down four enemy airplanes during World War II, including three in one day.

Below: At the 2008 Gathering of Eagles, Dr. Roscoe Brown, shown here with historian Dan Haulman, was honored as an aviation hero. Brown shot down a German jet on March 24, 1945, while flying with the 100th Fighter Squadron of the 332nd Fighter Group.

Above: Three of the original Tuskegee Airmen came to the Air Force Historical Agency in 2010 to help with research over the issue of the Airmen's bomber escort missions during World War II. Second, fourth, and fifth from left, respectively, are Airmen William Holloman, George Hardy, and Alexander Jefferson. With them are researcher Craig Huntly, left, and historian Daniel Haulman, center.

Right: Holloman (wearing his special "Red Tails" shirt) and William Ellis, right, were among the veterans at a Tuskegee Airmen convention in Philadelphia in 2008.

Chief of Staff of the Air Force Gen. Norton Schwartz, center, tries on his new Tuskegee Airmen jacket during a ceremony at the Pentagon on November 9, 2010, as retired Air Force Brigadier General Leon Johnson, left, the president of Tuskegee Airmen Incorporated, and Byron Morris, the president of Tuskegee Airmen Incorporated's East Coast Chapter, look on. Johnson presented Schwartz with an honorary Tuskegee Airmen membership, an honor bestowed on only two previous Air Force chiefs of staff.

President George W. Bush and Speaker of the House Nancy Pelosi stand amid a sea of Tuskegee Airmen veterans at the U.S. Capitol in Washington in March 2007. The occasion was the presentation by President Bush, on behalf of Congress, of the Congressional Gold Medal to the Tuskegee Airmen collectively for their service during World War II. Replicas of the medal were furnished to many of the Tuskegee Airmen in attendance or to family members of Airmen who were deceased or unable to attend in person.

9

CHRONOLOGY OF THE TUSKEGEE AIRMEN

KEY TO ABBREVIATIONS

FS	Fighter Squadron
PS	Pursuit Squadron
BS	Bombardment Squadron
BW	Bombardment Wing
FG	Fighter Group
TAAF	Tuskegee Army Air Field

1939

June 27: Congress passed the Civilian Pilot Training Act.

October: The Civil Aeronautics Authority approved Tuskegee Institute's application to be a civilian pilot training institution. The application was approved after Tuskegee obtained permission to use the nearby Montgomery Airport.

1940

Late February: The Civil Aeronautics Authority approved Tuskegee's Kennedy Field for Civilian Pilot Training, after improvements to the field, eliminating Tuskegee Institute's need to use the Montgomery Airport.

March 25: George A. Wiggs arrived in Tuskegee to administer the standard written examination required of all Civilian Pilot Training students. Every student who took the examination passed, surpassing the passing rate of other schools in the South.

September 16: Congress passed a Selective Service Act that required all the armed services to enlist "Negroes." The War Department announced that the Civil Aeronautics Authority, in cooperation with the U.S. Army, would start the training of "colored personnel" for the aviation service.

Late October: President Franklin D. Roosevelt's administration announced that blacks would be trained as military pilots in the Army Air Corps. The War Department promoted Benjamin O. Davis Sr. to be the first black general in the U.S. Army and Judge William H. Hastie, the first black federal judge, as a civilian advisor to Secretary of War Henry L. Stimson. All three actions were designed to discourage black voters from supporting Republican candidate Wendell Wilkie in the November 1940 presidential election.

Beneath the famous "Lifting the Veil" statue on the Tuskegee campus, the first class of aviation cadets entered training.

December 20: The War Department issued Army Regulation 210-10 that required post commanders to insure that all officers at an installation be allowed full membership in the officers' club or other social organization.

1941

January 16: The War Department announced plans to create a "Negro pursuit squadron" whose pilots would be trained at Tuskegee, Alabama.

March 19: The 99PS and a new "Air Base Detachment" were constituted.

March 22: The 99PS was activated at Chanute Field, Illinois, under the command of Capt Harold R. Maddux, a white officer, but composed of African American enlisted men.

Late March: Mrs. Eleanor Roosevelt, wife of President Franklin D. Roosevelt, visited Kennedy Field in the Tuskegee area and was taken up in an aircraft piloted by Chief C. Alfred Anderson, Tuskegee Institute's chief instructor pilot. Mrs. Roosevelt was a Rosenwald Fund trustee who helped secure financing for the construction of Moton Field at Tuskegee.

May 1: The "Air Base Detachment" was activated at Chanute Field, Illinois, to support the 99PS.

June 7: The War Department approved a contract that established a primary flying school at Tuskegee Institute. Capt Noel F. Parrish was assigned as one of the faculty members.

July 12: Construction began on TAAF, a military airfield a few miles northwest of Moton Field, which would provide basic and advanced military flight training for the pilots who had already received primary flight training at Moton Field.

July 19: The first class of aviation cadets (42-C) entered Preflight Training at Tuskegee Institute. It included Capt Benjamin Oliver Davis Jr., who served as Commandant of Cadets. Twelve cadets served with him under Capt Noel F. Parrish, a white officer, and 2nd Lt Harold C. Magoon, another white officer, who served as the adjutant. The other cadets were: John C. Anderson

First Lady Eleanor Roosevelt, center, gave a boost to the program when she toured the Tuskegee aviation training operations in March 1941.

Jr., Charles D. Brown, Theodore E. Brown, Marion A. Carter, Lemuel R. Custis, Charles H. De-Bow Jr., Frederick H. Moore, Ulysses S. Pannell, George S. Roberts, Mac Ross, William H. Slade, and Roderick C. Williams. Only five of these cadets completed the flying training at Tuskegee, in March 1942.

July 23: The Air Corps established an Air Corps Advanced Flying School to be activated at Tuskegee.

August 6: The Air Corps Advanced Flying School at Tuskegee was activated. It was later redesignated as the Tuskegee Advanced Flying School; the Army Air Forces Advanced Flying School; and the Army Air Forces Pilot School (Basic-Advanced).

August 21: The first class of aviation cadets entered the first phase of military flight training (Primary) administered by Tuskegee Institute, under contract with the War Department, at Kennedy Field near Tuskegee, because Moton Field was not yet completed.

November 5: The 99PS moved from Chanute Field, Illinois, to Maxwell Field, Alabama.

November 8: The first class of aviation cadets entered the second phase of military flight training (Basic) at TAAF, under military instructors. Only six of the 13 original cadets remained. Maj James A. Ellison was the first commander at TAAF.

November 10: The 99PS moved from Maxwell Field to TAAF, Alabama. 2nd Lt Clyde H. Bynum, a white officer, became its new commander. The Air Base Detachment moved from Chanute Field, Illinois, to Maxwell Field, Alabama, where the 99PS had been.

December: Maj Noel F. Parrish transferred from the Primary Flying School at Moton Field to the Air Corps Advanced Flying School at TAAF as Director of Training.

Lt. Col. Noel Parrish.

December 6: Capt Alonzo S. Ward became the third commander of the 99FS. Like the first two commanders of the unit, he was white.

December 7: The Japanese attacked Pearl Harbor in Hawaii, bringing the United States into World War II. The need for combat pilots skyrocketed.

December 27: The 100PS was constituted.

1942

January: Col Frederick V. H. Kimble replaced Maj James A. Ellison as commander at TAAF.

January 5: The "Air Base Detachment" that had served with the 99PS at Chanute Field, Illinois and then moved to Maxwell Field, Alabama on November 10, 1941 (when the 99PS moved to Tuskegee) moved from Maxwell to TAAF, Alabama. It would later be redesignated as the 318th Air Base Squadron and still later as the

318th Base Headquarters and Air Base Squadron (Colored).

January 11: Five of the aviation cadets at Tuskegee entered advanced flying training with P-40s. They soon deployed to Eglin Field, Florida, for gunnery practice.

February 19: The 100PS, which had been constituted on December 27, 1941, was activated at TAAF, Alabama. It was the second African American Army Air Forces unit ever to be activated.

March 7: The first class of African American pilots at TAAF completed advanced pilot training. There were only five who completed the training: Capt Benjamin O. Davis, Jr and 2nd Lts Mac Ross; Lemuel R. Custis; Charles H. DeBow Jr.; and George S. Roberts. Davis was assigned to the base, and the other four became the first African American flying officers in the 99PS. Capt Davis was the first black American to hold a regular commission in the nation's air arm, having transferred on graduation from the infantry to

A 1942 photo of Tuskegee Airmen-related dignitaries in front of the famous Booker T. Washington statue on the Tuskegee Institute campus. Seated from left are Cololnel B. O. Davis Jr., Major General Ralph Royce (commander of the AAF Southeast Training Center), Tuskegee Institute President Frederick Patterson, and Colonel Noel Parrish.

Moton Field under construction, August 1942.

the Army Air Corps.

March 13: The "Air Base Detachment" at Tuskegee was redesignated as the 318th Air Base Squadron.

March 21: The 96th Maintenance Group (Reduced) (Colored) was activated at TAAF, Alabama. The 366th and 367th Materiel Squadrons were activated under the 96th Maintenance Group.

April 14: A Factory Training School associated with the Curtiss Wright Service School, Williamsville Branch, was activated in Buffalo, New York. It would later train African American P-40 airplane mechanics.

April 17: The Air Corps Advanced Flying School at TAAF was redesignated as Tuskegee Advanced Flying School.

April 29: The second class of African American pilots graduated from flying training at TAAF.

May 15: The 99PS was redesignated as the 99FS and the 100PS was redesignated as the 100FS.

May 20: The third class of African American pilots graduated from flying training at TAAF.

June 1: 1st Lt George S. Roberts assumed command of the 99 FS. He was the first African American to command the squadron.

June 13: the 318th Air Base Squadron at Tuskegee was redesignated as the 318th Base Headquarters and Air Base Squadron (Colored). It served with the 99FS at Tuskegee.

July 3: The fourth class of African American pilots graduated from flying training at TAAF.

July 4: The 332FG was constituted. The 301 and 302FSs were also constituted, for eventual assignment to the group.

July 25: The 96th Maintenance Group was redesignated as the 96th Service Group at TAAF. The 366th and 367th Materiel Squadrons were redesignated as the 366th and 367th Service Squadrons at Tuskegee.

August 5: The fifth class of African American pilots graduated from flying training at TAAF. Enough African American pilots had completed training to bring the 99FS to its full strength of 33 pilots.

August 19: The 99FS was attached to the III Fighter Command.

August 22: Lt Col Benjamin O. Davis Jr. became commander of the 99FS, replacing Lt George S. Roberts in that position. Col Davis was the second black commander of the unit.

August 27: The War Department organized the Advisory Committee on Negro Troop Policies, with Assistant Secretary of War John J. McCloy as chairman.

September 6: The sixth class of African American pilots graduated from flying training at TAAF.

September 12: Lt Faythe A. McGinnis crashed on a routine flight and became the first casualty of the 99FS.

September 15: The 1000th Signal Company, the 1051st Quartermaster Service Group Aviation Company, the 1765th Ordnance Supply and Maintenance Company, Aviation, and the 1901st and 1902nd Quartermaster Truck Company (Aviation) were all activated at TAAF.

September: After further gunnery training at Eglin and Dale Mabry Fields in Florida, the 99FS returned to Tuskegee and was declared ready for combat. However, its planned deployment to defend Liberia was indefinitely delayed because of

Alice Dungey Gray headed the parachute rigging department at Tuskegee AAF.

the diminished enemy threat to North Africa.

October 7: Secretary of War Henry L. Stimson visited the 99FS at TAAF.

October 9: The seventh class of African American pilots graduated from flying training at TAAF.

October 13: The 332FG was activated at TAAF, Alabama, and the pre-existing 100FS was assigned to it. The 301 and 302 FSs were also activated for the first time at Tuskegee, and assigned to the 332FG. This group was the first African American group in the Army Air Forces. Eventually, all four of the African American squadrons in the Army Air Forces were assigned to the 332FG. The 332 Fighter Control Squadron (Colored) was activated at TAAF.

October 19: Lt Col Sam W. Westbrook Jr. became commander of the 332FG. He was a white officer.

November 10: The eighth class of African American pilots graduated from flying training at TAAF.

November 12: 1st Lt Charles W. Walker became the first black officer assigned to the 332FG. He was a chaplain.

November 17: Lt Col Benjamin O. Davis Jr. addressed the assembled 99FS.

November 23: The 99FS paraded for the first time.

December: Lt Col Noel F. Parrish, who had served as Director of Training at the Tuskegee Advanced Flying School, became commanding officer of the school, replacing Col Frederick Kimble. Parrish allowed more desegregation of the facilities on the field than his predecessors.

December 13: The ninth class of African American

Tuskegee Field on an approach to the northwest runway.

pilots graduated from flying training at TAAF.

December 22: The 99FS deployed to Dale Mabry Field, Florida, for maneuvers.

1943

January 15: The emblem of the 332FG was approved. On a blue shield with a gold band across the middle, a black panther breathing fire.

January 26: The 366th and 367th Service Squadrons and the 43nd Medical Support Platoon,

Aviation were all assigned to the 96th Service Group at Tuskegee.

January 30: Lt Richard A. Davis crashed, becoming the second casualty of the 99FS.

Feb 9: Six 99FS pilots engaged in a mock dogfight with six other pilots, for practice.

March 15: The 332nd Fighter Control Squadron (Colored) was disbanded at TAAF.

March 24: Lt Earl E. King became the third casualty of the 99FS.

March 26: The 332FG and its 100, 301, and 302FSs

departed Tuskegee Army Air Base for another field.

March 29: The 332FG completed its move from TAAF, Alabama, to Selfridge Field, Michigan.

April 2: The 99FS departed TAAF, Alabama, for movement overseas for combat operations.

April 4: The 99FS arrived at Camp Shanks, New York, in preparation for deployment overseas for combat. The 96th Service Group completed its move to Selfridge Field, Michigan, in order to serve with the 332FG.

April 12: The 332FG moved from Selfridge Field to Oscoda, Michigan.

April 16: The 99FS sailed aboard the steamship *Mariposa* from New York harbor, bound eastward across the Atlantic Ocean for Africa.

April 24: The 99FS arrived at Casablanca, French Morocco, its first overseas base, and began serving the Twelfth Air Force.

April 25: The 320th College Training Detachment (Aircrew) was activated at Tuskegee Institute, Alabama.

April 29: The 99FS moved to Oued N'ja, French Morocco. There it engaged in maneuvers and prepared for combat.

May 5: Lts James T. Wiley and Graham Smith were the first two P-40 pilots of the 99FS to land in North Africa, at Oued N'ja, French Morocco.

May 9: Personnel of the 99FS took part in a parade in Fez, French Morocco to celebrate the liberation of Tunisia. Capt Hayden C. Johnson led the squadron contingent in the ceremony.

May 13: Enemy forces in Tunisia surrendered, leaving all North Africa under Allied control.

May 16: Col Robert R. Selway Jr. became commander of the 332FG back in the United States. Like his predecessor, he was a white officer.

May 19: Lt Gen Carl Spaatz, commander of the Twelfth Air Force, inspected the flying field of the 99FS at Oued N'ja.

May 28: The 99FS was assigned to the XII Air Support (later, XII Tactical Air) Command.

May 29: The 99FS was attached to the 33FG, which was under the command of Col William M. Momyer.

June 2: The 99FS flew its first combat mission, flying P-40 aircraft on patrol over the Mediterranean while attached to the 332FG.

June 2-9: The 99FS flew an average of two Italian missions daily for the 99FS during the campaign against Pantelleria Island, which ended on 11 June. Some of the missions targeted enemy gun sites on the Italian island, and some escorted A-20 and B-25 aircraft on raids against enemy targets there.

June 7: The 99FS moved to Fardjouna, Tunisia, from which base it took part with other units in air raids on Pantelleria.

June 9: The 99FS encountered enemy aircraft for the first time during a mission on which it escorted 12 A-20s over Pantelleria Island. Four of the P-40s of the squadron intercepted four Me-109 German fighters and the enemy fled. P-40s of another squadron escorted the A-20s home.

June 10: The 96th Service Group moved from Selfridge Field to Oscoda Field, Michigan, to which the 332FG had moved in April.

June 11: The surrender of enemy forces on Pantelleria paved the way for the Allied invasion of Sicily.

June 15: The 99FS flew four missions in one day, to cover Allied shipping.

June 18: The 99FS encountered enemy aircraft for the second time, and 1st Lt Lee Rayford's P-40 was hit several times.

c. June 29: The 99FS was attached to the 324FG, under the command of Col William K. McNown, and began flying escort missions between Tunisia and Sicily.

June: During this month, King George VI of the British Empire visited Grombalia Airfield in North Africa and reviewed approximately 50 enlisted men of the 99FS. The 789th Technical School Squadron at Lincoln, Nebraska, graduated its first class of African American fighter mechanics.

July 2: While escorting B-25 medium bombers on a raid on Castelvetrano in southwestern Sicily, Italy, 1st Lt Charles B. Hall of the 99FS earned the first Tuskegee Airmen aerial victory credit by shooting down an FW-190 German aircraft. Lt W. I. Lawson also claimed probable destruction of another FW-190 and damaged an Me-109. 1st Lt Sherman W. White and 2nd Lt James L. McCullin were the first Tuskegee Airmen lost in combat. Although both went missing, one is believed to have landed on enemy-held Sicily. That afternoon, Gen Dwight D. Eisenhower also visited the 99FS.

July 3: The 99FS joined three other fighter squadrons of the 324FG, to which it was attached, in escorting medium bombers to Sicily. During that mission, enemy fighters shot down at least one of the bombers.

June-July: The 99FS earned the first of its three World War II Distinguished Unit Citations for missions over Sicily. The unit provided air support for Allied landing operations and for Allied offensives on the island. The 324FG, to which the 99FS was attached, also earned the award.

July 6: Air Vice Marshal Sir Arthur Coningham of the Royal Air Force, who commanded the North African Tactical Air Force, visited the 99FS at Fardjouna.

1st Lt Sherman White was killed July 2, 1943.

July 8: The 99FS escorted medium bombers to Milo, Sicily.

July 9: The 332FG moved from Oscoda, Michigan, back to Selfridge Field, Michigan, but the 96th Service Group, which maintained the airplanes, remained at Oscoda.

July 10: During the invasion of Sicily, the 99FS covered the landing of Allied troops at Licata.

July 11: The 99FS drove off 12 German FW-190 fighters attempting to attack Allied naval vessels in the Mediterranean. 1st Lt George R. Bolling was hit by antiaircraft artillery coming from some of the vessels and bailed out. He later returned to the squadron after being rescued by boat.

July 19: The 99FS was attached again to the 33FG, under Col William W. Momyer. It provided cover for Allied shipping in the Mediterranean and air support for the Seventh Army. 29 C-47 transport planes helped carry personnel and equipment of the 99FS to Licata, Sicily.

July 21: The 99FS flew 13 missions in one day.

July 23: The first three replacement pilots arrived for the 99FS. They included Lts Howard L. Baugh, Edward L. Toppins, and Morgan (first name not given).

July 23: Tuskegee Advanced Flying School, at TAAF, Alabama, was redesignated as AAF Pilot School (Basic-Advanced).

July 26: The 99FS flew 12 missions in one day.

July 27: Maj Gen Edwin J. House, commander of the XII Air Support Command of the Twelfth Air Force, visited the 99FS

July 28: The 99FS moved from Tunisia in North Africa to Licata, Sicily. Lt Col Benjamin O. Davis Jr. and 1st Lt Herbert Carter of the 99FS flew to

Enlisted mechanics stand on P-40 wings as aviation cadets pass in review during a Saturday parade at Tuskegee Army Air Field, August 9, 1943.

Tunis to meet with Secretary of War Henry L. Stimson.

July 28: Raymond Cassagnol of Haiti became the first foreign cadet to graduate from pilot training at TAAF.

June-July: The 99FS earned its first Distinguished Unit Citation for missions over Sicily during the period June-July 1943.

August 11: Lt Paul G. Mitchell was killed when his airplane crashed in mid-air with another airplane in his formation. He was the third 99FS pilot lost in combat.

August 15: Brig Gen John K. Cannon, commander of Northwest African Training Command, visited the 99FS.

August 17: The Sicilian campaign ended.

August 24: The 99FS received six replacement pilots from the United States.

September 2: Maj George S. Roberts replaced Lt Col Benjamin O. Davis as commander of the 99FS as Davis began a return trip to the United States, where he would assume command of the 332FG. Maj Roberts had been the first black

commander of the unit before Col Davis. He had been serving as the squadron's operations officer.

September 4: The 99FS moved to Termini, Sicily.

September 11: Advance elements of the 99FS landed on a beach at Battapaglia in Italy, under enemy fire.

September 13: The first class of liaison pilots graduated at TAAF. They would eventually be assigned to U.S. Army ground organizations, but fly liaison airplanes in their support.

September 16: Maj Gen Edwin J. House, commander of the XII Air Support Command, sent a memorandum to Maj Gen John K. Cannon, Deputy Commander of the Northwest African Tactical Air Force, regarding the "Combat Efficiency of the 99FS". The letter criticized the black squadron as performing poorly in combat, based partly on information supplied by Col William Momyer, commander of the 33FG, to which the 99FS was attached. The report recommended that the squadron trade in its P-40s for P-39s and be assigned to coastal patrols. It also recommended that a black fighter group not be deployed overseas for combat.

September 17: The 99FS moved to Barcellona, Sicily. 1st Lt Sidney P. Brooks crashed, and died the next day, Tuskegee's fourth pilot lost in combat.

September 18: Responding to the memorandum from Maj Gen House of the XII Air Support Command, Maj Gen J. K. Cannon, deputy commander of the Northwest African Tactical Air Force, prepared a memorandum for the commanding general of the Northwest African Air Force critical of the 99FS.

September 19: Lt Gen Carl Spaatz, commander of the Northwest African Air Forces, and commander of the Twelfth Air Force, prepared a memo as he forwarded the memoranda from

Gens House and Cannon on the combat performance of the 99FS. Spaatz expressed his "full confidence in the fairness of the analysis made by both Gen Cannon and Gen House." He also noted that he had personally inspected the 99FS several times, and found that "there has been no question of their ground discipline and their general conduct. It has been excellent." He noted that "In processing them for combat action they were given the benefit of our training system of the supervision of instructors with much combat experience. They were processed into combat action very carefully." Spaatz forwarded the memoranda and his own note to the commanding general, Army Air Forces, who was Gen Henry "Hap" Arnold, in Washington, D.C.

September: During this month, German forces bombarded and strafed the base of the 99FS for five consecutive days and nights, but there were no squadron casualties.

September 20: *Time* magazine published an article called "Experiment Proved?" regarding the combat performance of the 99FS, the only black Army Air Forces squadron in combat, which included comments of its commander, Col Benjamin O. Davis Jr. Although the article mentioned that the squadron "seems to have done fairly well," it also noted that the Army Air Forces was considering reducing its combat role to coastal patrol duty.

September 23: 99FS airplanes landed on the Italian mainland for the first time, but the main base remained at Barcellona, Sicily.

October 8: Col Benjamin O. Davis Jr., who had served as commander of the 99FS in combat in North Africa and Italy, became the first black commander of the 332FG, replacing Col Robert R. Selway Jr. Both Selway and Davis were graduates of the U.S. Military Academy at West Point.

October 13: The Report on the Combat Efficiency of the 99FS, prepared by Maj Gen Edwin J. House of the XII Air Support Command, based in part on information from Col William Momyer, commander of the 33FG, and endorsed by Maj Gen John K. Cannon, Deputy Commander of the Mediterranean Allied Tactical Air Force and Lt Gen Carl Spaatz, commander of the Twelfth Air Force, was presented to the War Department's Advisory Committee on Negro Troop Policies. The report recommended a reduced combat role for the 99FS, based on a perception of poor performance.

October 16: Col Benjamin O. Davis Jr. met with members of the War Department's Advisory Committee on Negro Troop Policies and answered questions about the combat performance of the 99FS he had led. Col Davis defended the unit's record, and recommended that it be allowed to remain in combat. The War Department detached the 99FS from Col William Momyer's 33FG and attached it instead to the 79FG, under the command of Col Earl E. Bates Jr. As the 99FS served with the 79FG, perceptions of its combat performance improved.

October 17: The 99FS moved to Foggia, Italy. From that base it provided close air support for Allied ground troops and attacked surface targets such as ammunition dumps and enemy shipping.

November 1: Fifty P-38s landed at Sal Solo Field in Italy, where mechanics of the 99FS serviced them.

November 5: Lts William A. Campbell, Span Watson, and Herbert V. Clark of the 99FS departed for the United States after having served their combat time overseas.

November 7: Maj Gen John K. Cannon, now commander of the XII Air Support Command, visited the 79FG and presented Air Medals to members of the 99FS who were attached to the group.

November 15: The AAF Pilot School (Basic-Advanced) at TAAF was assigned to the 28th Flying Training Wing, headquartered in Selma, Alabama.

November 22: The 99FS moved to Madna, Italy.

November 29: After several days of not flying missions, the 99FS flew five this day.

November 30-31: The 99FS took part with the 79FG in attacks on ground targets in support of Field Marshall Bernard Montgomery's crossing of the Sangro River in Italy.

December 5: The first class of twin-engine pilots graduated at TAAF. They would eventually fly B-25 bombers with the 477BG.

December 9: Gen Henry H. Arnold, commander of the Army Air Forces, visited the 99FS at Madna Airfield, Italy, accompanied by Lt Gen Carl Spaatz, commander of the Twelfth Air Force, and Maj Gen John Cannon, deputy commander of the Mediterranean Allied Tactical Air Force.

December 22: The 332FG departed Selfridge Field, Michigan, for movement overseas. Meanwhile, in Italy, Lt James Wiley of Pittsburgh became the first 99FS pilot to complete 50 sorties.

December: The 99FS flew many missions while attached to the 79FG to provide close air cover for ground troops of the British Eighth Army in Italy.

1944

January: The 79FG included several pilots of the 99FS among its own squadrons on certain missions.

January 2: 1 Lt John H. Morgan of the 99FS died while serving overseas.

January 3: 332FG and its three fighter squadrons, the 100th, 301st, and 302nd, departed Hampton Roads, Virginia, on four ships in a convoy to cross the Atlantic. The 332FG voyaged on the SS *William Few* (HR-814). Squadrons of the group traveled on other ships in the convoy. The 100FS sailed aboard the SS *John M. Morehead* (HR-810); the 301FS sailed aboard the SS *Clark Mills* (HR-812); and the 30 FS sailed aboard the SS *Thomas B. Robertson* (HR-811). The 96th Service Group departed Hampton Roads Port of Embarkation, Virginia, for overseas duty. It sailed on ship 6122 (USS *Josiah Bartlett*) for the Mediterranean Sea. The 96th Service Group's 366th and 367th Air Service Squadrons also sailed on the same ship.

January 15: The 477BG, Medium, was activated again at Selfridge Field, Michigan, along with the 616BS. The group was equipped with B-25 medium bombers. Meanwhile, back in Italy, 2nd Lt William E. Griffin of the 99FS was seen to go down during a dive bombing mission to the town of S. Valentino and was listed as missing in action.

January 16: The 99FS moved from Madna to Capodichino Airdrome near Naples, Italy. From there it began flying coastal patrol missions south of Rome.

January 21: Col Robert R. Selway Jr., a white officer who had commanded the 332FG from May 16 to Oct 8, 1943, became commander of the 477BG.

January 27: Capt Clarence C. Jamison, while leading a formation of 16 fighters of the 99FS, spotted 15 FW-190s dive-bombing shipping off St. Peter's Beach near Anzio. During the ensuing engagement, 10 members of the 99th shot down a total of 10 enemy airplanes. The victors included 2nd Lt Clarence W. Allen (.5 credits), 1st Lt Willie Ashley Jr. (1 credit), 2nd Lt Charles P. Bailey (1 credit), 1 Lt Howard Baugh (1.5 credits), Capt Lemuel R. Custis (1 credit), 1st Lt Robert W. Deiz (1 credit), 2nd Lt Wilson V. Eagleson (1 credit), 1st Lt Leon C. Roberts (1 credit), 2nd Lt

Lewis C. Smith (1 credit), 1st Lt Edward L. Toppins (1 credit). All of the downed enemy airplanes were Germana FW-190s. Lt Samuel F. Bruce was killed in aerial combat with enemy FW-190s. He bailed out but his chute, did not fill.

January 28: Following up the previous day's aerial victories, two members of the 99FS shot down a total of three enemy airplanes that threatened American ground forces of the Fifth Army at Anzio. The victors were Capt Charles B. Hall, who had been the first Tuskegee Airman to shoot down an enemy airplane, and Lt Robert W. Deiz. Capt Hall shot down two aircraft, raising his total to three. For his actions on this day, Hall earned the Distinguished Flying Cross. In two days, January 27-28, 1944, the Tuskegee Airmen shot down a total of 13 enemy airplanes over Anzio, Italy. The 96th Service Group arrived in North Africa. A multi-ship convoy carrying the 332FG and the 100, 301, and 302FSs arrived in North Africa on the way to Italy.

February 1-3: After having crossed the Atlantic from Virginia, ships carrying the 332FG and its three squadrons, the 100th, 301st, and 302nd arrived at the mainland of Italy after stopping briefly in North Africa and Sicily on the way. The organizations debarked at Bari, Taranto, and Naples, Italy. During the same week, the 96th Air Service Group debarked at Bari, Italy.

February 2: The 99FS dive-bombed a key bridge in the Anzio area to prevent escape of the enemy.

February 3: The 332FG's 100FS arrived at Mon-

Capt Charles W. Brooks, medical officer for the 196th Squadron.

tecorvino, Italy, the group's first overseas base of operations.

February 5: The 332FG's 100FS began flying P-39s in Italy, but not yet on combat missions. The group flew with the 62FW. Lt Elwood T. Driver, flying a P-40 for the 99FS (not yet assigned to the 332FG), shot down one FW-190.

February 7: Three Tuskegee Airmen of the 99FS, flying P-40s, shot down three German FW-190s. The victors included 1st Lt Clinton B. Mills and 2nd Lt Wilson V. Eagleson and Leonard M. Jackson. All of the downed enemy airplanes were FW-190s. The 302FS arrived at Montecorvino, where the 100FS was already stationed.

February 8: The 301FS arrived at Montecorvino, Italy, where the 100 and 302FSs were already stationed. All three of the 332FG's squadrons were then stationed at the same base. Meanwhile, P-40s of the 99FS escorted a transport aircraft carrying Lt Gen Mark Clark, commander of the Fifth Army, on a flight in Italy.

February 10: The 96 Air Service Group arrived at Montecorvino to serve there with the 332FG.

February 15: The 332FG's 301FS entered combat

An Army band performing for an officers' dance in 1944.

for the first time. Within days, all three of the group's squadrons, including the 100 and 302FS, had also flown combat missions.

February 21: The 100FS moved to Capodichino, Italy, but the other three squadrons of the 332FG remained with group headquarters at Montecorvino. The squadrons would not all be located at the same base again until mid-April. Meanwhile, the 99FS, not yet assigned to the 332FG, flew four patrol missions. 2nd Lt Alwayne M. Dunlap of the 99th was killed in an aircraft crash after overshooting his landing field. 2nd Lt Pearlee E. Saunders was wounded after crash landing his P-40, and Lt Herbert Carter's airplane was hit by flak.

February 23 or 24: 2nd Lt Harry J. Daniels of the 332FG's 301FS was reported missing after flying into bad weather. He was the first 332FG pilot reported to have been killed overseas.

February 29: 2nd Lt George T. McCrumby of the 99FS went missing in action after reporting engine trouble, and his body was later found.

February: During this month, the 99FS flew 55 missions, mostly dive-bombing, but also patrol, while attached to the 79FG of the Twelfth Air Force.

March 6: The 302FS moved from Montecorvino to Capodichino, Italy, where the 100FS had already moved, but the 332FG headquarters, and the 301FS, remained at Montecorvino.

March 6: In a letter to Maj Gen Barney Giles at Headquarters, Army Air Forces, Maj Gen Ira C. Eaker, commander of the Mediterranean Allied Air Forces, recommended that the 332FG be equipped with P-47 fighters instead of P-39s so that the group could begin to escort heavy bombers as its primary mission. However, the group had to wait until June to begin flying heavy bomber escort missions for the Fifteenth Air Force.

March 9: Lt Wayne Vincent Liggins of the 301FS was killed while on a training mission. His engine failed. Meanwhile, in the 99FS, not yet assigned to the 332FG, 2nd Lt John Hamilton was wounded in the leg by flak during a dive-bombing mission in the Anzio area.

March 13: The 99FS flew three missions. The first of these dive-bombed two heavy gun positions with 1000-pound bombs, with five hits recorded.

March 15: The 99FS flew two dive-bombing missions on targets in the Monte Cassino area of Italy.

March 16-17: The 99FS temporarily acquired three P-47 fighter aircraft and began transition training with them, but continued to fly P-40 aircraft in combat.

March 18: 2nd Lt Clemenceau McAdoo Givings of the 100FS was killed on a routine flying mission when his plane crashed into the sea. Meanwhile, the 99FS, in another part of Italy, witnessed the eruption of Mount Vesuvius.

March 22: The eruption of Mount Vesuvius near Naples, Italy, spread ash over the 332FG at Montecorvino.

March 30: The Statistical Control Division, Office of Management Control, issued a report on "Operations of the 99FS Compared with Other P-40 Aircraft Squadrons in the MTO (Mediterranean Theater of Operations), July 3, 1943-January 31, 1944." The report noted that the black 99FS had performed as well as other squadrons with which it served, implying that the letter of Gen House dated September 16, 1943, which had called the squadron inferior, had been wrong.

March 31: 2nd Lt Norvel Stoudmire was killed while flying on a harbor patrol mission. His aircraft caught on fire, and he was not able to bail out safely.

March: During the month of March 1944, the 99FS flew 39 missions, mostly dive-bombing enemy targets.

April 1: The 99FS was attached again to the 324FG after having been attached for months to the 79FG. The commander of the 324FG at the time was Col Leonard C. Lydon. Some of the squadron members complained about the move, since they had grown to like their association with the 79FG.

April 2: The 99FS moved to Cercola, Italy. It had been one year since the squadron departed Tuskegee.

April 4: The 99FS flew its first mission from Cercola, while attached to the 324FG, also stationed there.

April 10: The 115th AAF Base Unit was organized at Selfridge Field, Michigan, home of the 477BG.

April 13: Capt Erwin B. Lawrence Jr. replaced Maj George B. Roberts as commander of the 99FS. Maj Roberts was planning to return to the United States for rest and recuperation, but would eventually command the squadron again, for a third time.

April 15: The 332FG and the 301FS moved from Montecorvino, Italy, to Capodichino, Italy, to which the 100 and 302FSs had already moved. For the first time since early February 1944, when the 332FG and its three squadrons were all stationed at Montecorvino, the units were all co-located. Back in the United States, the 617BS was activated again and assigned to the 477BG, Medium.

April 19: Maj George S. Roberts, Capt Lemuel R

Weather officer giving pilots last-minute changes.

Custis, and Capt Herbert Carter bade farewell to the enlisted personnel of the 99FS as they prepared to return to the United States. Maj Roberts and Capt Custis had been with the squadron since its beginning. Other squadron personnel departing were Capts Charles B. Hall, who had scored the squadron's first aerial victory, and James T. Wiley; Lts Willie Ashley and Willie Fuller. 2nd Lt Beryl Wyatt of the 100FS died from injuries suffered in an aircraft crash.

April 20: Lt Gen Ira C. Eaker, Commanding General, Mediterranean Allied Air Forces, visited the 332FG in Italy. Lt Ray B. Ware, the 332FG public relations officer, announced that the group would soon be converting from P-39 to P-47 aircraft and move to the east coast of Italy, presumably for bomber escort duty. Later that day, Gen Eaker, accompanied by Lt Col Benjamin O. Davis Jr., commander of the 332FG, visited the 99FS. The 99FS, which Col Davis had commanded earlier, would eventually be assigned to the 332FG for

the bomber escort duty.

April 24: 2nd Lt Edgar L. Jones was killed in an aircraft crash on takeoff for a strafing mission. That night, thirty to forty German JU-88 airplanes raided the 332FG area, wounding one enlisted man, Staff Sergeant Alvin H. Kent, who earned the Purple Heart.

April 25: The 332FG received its first six P-47 airplanes, two of which were assigned to each of the group's fighter squadrons, the 100th, 301st, and 302nd. P-47s eventually replaced all of the P-39 fighters the group had flown.

April 30: The 320th College Training Detachment (Aircrew) was disbanded at Tuskegee Institute, Alabama. The 318th Base Headquarters and Air Base Squadron (Colored) at TAAF were disbanded. Personnel of the 318th transferred to the 2143nd Army Air Forces Base Unit.

April: The 99FS flew 32 missions, mostly dive-bombing enemy targets.

May 1: The 99FS in Italy was assigned to the 332FG but remained attached to the 324FG for combat operations. Back at TAAF in Alabama, the 2143nd AAF Base Unit was activated. It operated the pilot school for basic and advanced training there.

May 5: Lt James R. Polkinghorne Jr. of the 301FS was reported lost with his P-39 near Teragina, Italy. The cause was unknown.

May 6: An advance party of the 99FS moved to Pignataro Airfield in Italy. Back in the United States, the 477BG, Medium, moved from Selfridge Field, Michigan, to Godman Field, Kentucky. The 115th AAF Base Unit moved from Selfridge Field to Godman Field along with the 477BG with which it served.

May 10: The main body of the 99FS moved to Pignataro, Italy.

May 12: Capt Howard L. Baugh of the 99FS earned the Distinguished Flying Cross for his heroism on a mission on this date.

May 12-14: The 99FS earned its second Distinguished Unit Citation for missions over Monte Cassino, Italy, an honor it shared with the 324FG to which it was attached.

May 15: Back in the United States, the 618BS was activated again and assigned to the 477BG, Medium.

May 21: 1st Lt Charles W. Tate of the 99FS earned the Distinguished Flying Cross for his heroic actions on this date.

May 22: The 332FG transferred from the Twelfth Air Force to the Fifteenth Air Force It came under the operational control of the 306th Fighter Wing, which administered the fighter groups of the Fifteenth Air Force. The commander of the 306th Fighter Wing at the time was Brig Gen Dean C. Strother. The 96th Air Service Group was assigned from the Twelfth to the Fifteenth Air Force. 2 Lt Henry Pollard Jr. of the 302FS died while serving overseas.

May 24: 1st Lt John H. Prowell of the 301FS was reported lost with his P-39 over the Mediterranean, with possible engine failure.

May 27: 1st Lt Clarence W. Dart of the 99FS in Italy earned the Distinguished Flying Cross for his heroism on this date. The 99FS reported losing 2nd Lt James B. Brown and his P-40 near Prossinone, Italy. The cause was not known. Back in the United States, the 619BS was activated again and assigned to the 477BG, Medium. The group

now had all of its original squadrons active again under it, this time at Godman Field, Kentucky.

May 28: The 332FG moved from Capodichino to Ramitelli Airfield, Italy, where it would remain for the rest of the war in Europe.

May 29: The 96th Air Service Group was assigned to the Fifteenth Air Force Service Command of the Fifteenth Air Force.

June 2: The 99FS celebrated the first anniversary of its first combat mission and flew its 500th combat mission, led by squadron commander Capt Erwin B. Lawrence. Meanwhile, MSgt. William M. Harris, line chief, of the 302FS of the 332FG, was killed during an aircraft take-off. 2nd Lt Elmer Taylor, a pilot also of the 302FS, was killed in a crash during a training mission.

June 4: Capts Edward L. Toppins and Leonard M. Jackson, both of the 99FS earned the Distinguished Flying Cross for heroic actions on this date.

June 5: Capt Elwood T. Driver of the 99FS earned the Distinguished Flying Cross for his heroic actions on this date. The 99FS was detached from the 324FG. The 96th Air Service Group arrived at Foggia, Italy, very near Ramitelli, to provide services for the 332FG. Serving under the 96th Air Service Group were the 366th Service Squadron at Ramitelli and the 367th Service Squadron, at first at Foggia and later at Vasto and Falconara.

June 6: Lt Leonard M. Jackson crash-landed on no-man's land between enemy and Allied lines. He returned the next day with two captured Germans.

June 7: The 332FG flew its first mission, a sweep of the Ferrara-Bologna area, with the Fifteenth Air Force. 2nd Lt Carroll N. Langston Jr. of the 301FS was reported lost with his P-47 near San Benedetti, Italy. The cause was probable engine failure. On the same mission, Capt Lee Rayford

Above: 1st Lieutenant Charles Z. Clarke, (left) shows Group Information-Education Officer and First Sergeant Harts M. Brown of Headquarters Squadron, 96th Service Group, the money that was collected from enlisted men of the squadron for the Christmas Fund going to the Riverdale Orphanage, New York.

was wounded by flak. Meanwhile, the 99FS, not yet flying with the 332FG, flew four four-ship strafing missions to destroy 24 motor vehcles, damage 47 others, and destroy one self-propelled gun, with no friendly aircraft lost.

June 8: The 332FG flew its first heavy bomber escort mission, protecting B-17s of the 5BW on a mission to Pola, Italy. Meanwhile, 1st Lt Lewis C. Smith bailed out of his plane and went missing after being hit by flak on a dive-bombing mission with the 99FS, which had not yet joined the 332FG for bomber escort.

June 9: The 332FG escorted B-24s and B-17s of the 5, 47, 49, 55, and 304BWs on a raid to Munich, Germany, the group's first mission over Germany. Four Tuskegee Airmen shot down a total of five enemy Me-109 airplanes. The victors included 2nd Lt Frederick D. Funderburg, who shot down two Me-109s, and 1st Lt Charles M. Bussy, Melvin T. Jackson, and Wendell O. Pruitt, who each shot down one Me-109. These were the first aerial victories of the 332FG. For this mission, group commander Col Benjamin O. Davis Jr. earned a Distinguished Flying Cross for so skillfully handling his squadrons that "only a few bombers were lost." Enemy airplanes actually shot down only two B-24s of the escorted wing's 459BG during the time the 332FG was escorting them. This was the first time 332FG-escorted bombers fell to enemy airplanes. The losses were very understandable, given the fact that the number of bombers far exceeded the number of escort fighters to cover them. The group reported 2nd Lt Cornelius G. Rogers of the 301FG lost with his P-47D to an unknown cause near Pols, Italy.

June 11: The 99FS moved to Ciampino, Italy. and was attached to the 86FG under Col Harold E. Kofahl, but remained assigned to the 332FG. The 332FG, from which the 99FS was then detached, escorted B-17 and B-24 bombers of the 5 and 55BWs to the Smedervo area.

June 13: The 332FG escorted B-17 and B-24 bombers of the 5th and 49BWs to the Munich area. Enemy fighters shot down one of the B-24s over northern Italy.

June 14: The 332FG escorted B-17 and B-24 bombers on a mission to the Budapest area of Hungary. 2nd Lt Roger D. Brown of the 100FS was reported missing, along with his P-47 airplane, southeast of Ramitelli Air Base, Italy after experiencing engine trouble on a training flight. Meanwhile, over in the 99FS, Lt C. W. Allen went missing on a dive-bombing mission. He returned two days later after evading the enemy.

June 15: The 99FS flew six dive-bombing missions.

June 16: For the second day in a row, the 99FS flew six dive-bombing missions. Meanwhile, the 332FG escorted Fifteenth Air Force heavy bombers to the Bratislava area of Slovakia.

June 17: The 99FS moved to Orbetello, Italy.

June 23: The 332FG escorted Fifteenth Air Force heavy bombers to the Bucharest-Giurgiu area of Rumania.

June 24: P-47 fighters of the 332FG strafed Airasca-Pinerole landing ground. Capt Robert B. Tresville Jr., 2nd Lt Samuel Jefferson, and 2nd Lt Charles B. Johnson, all of the 100FS, were reported missing, one near the northern coast of Italy, and another off Corsica in the Mediterranean Sea. Capt Tresville was a graduate of the U.S. Military Academy at West Point. The emblem of the 99FS, consisting of a gold winged diving panther on a blue disk, with a background of nine stars, four above and five below the panther., was approved.

June 25: In the morning, eight P-47 pilots of the 332FG, including 2nd Lt Gwynne W. Pierson of the 302FS, strafed a German warship in the Adriatic Sea (Gulf of Venice) near Pirano not far from Trieste, then in Italy. They reported the ship was a German destroyer and that it was sunk. The ship was probably the TA-22, which had been converted into a German torpedo boat from the captured Italian warship *Giuseppe Missori*. The 240-foot-long ship might have appeared to be a German destroyer. No other German warship was reported hit by Allied aircraft that day, and the time and place agree. The TA-22 suffered so much damage that it was permanently taken out of service. It was reported scuttled off Trieste on May 3, 1945.

June 26: The 332FG flew a bomber escort mission to the Lake Balaton area of Hungary. Capt Andrew Maples Jr. and 1st Lt Maurice V. Esters, both of the 301FS, suffered engine failure or mechanical trouble, and bailed out of their P-47D airplanes.

June 27: The 332FG escorted B-17 bombers of the 5BW and B-24 bombers of the 47BW to the Budapest area of Hungary and reported no losses.

June 28: The 332FG escorted B-17 bombers of the 304BW to the Ferdinand area. Lt Edward Laird of the 100FS crashed and was killed on takeoff. 2nd Lt Othel Dickson of the 301FS was also killed in a crash, while on a transition mission. The 99FS received orders to move to Ramitelli Air Field, Italy, where the 332FG was already based.

June 29: 2nd Lt Floyd A. Thompson of the 99FS was hit by flak and bailed out of his plane, landing near Spescia, Italy. The 99FS began transferring the best of its P-40 aircraft to the 324FG, in anticipation of its move to Ramitelli.

June 30: The 332FG escorted heavy bombers of the Fifteenth Air Force to the Vienna, Austria area (then part of greater Germany). Five of the bombers were shot down by enemy aircraft, but probably after the 332FG's escort duty had finished. The 99FS transferred most of its remaining P-40 fighter aircraft and prepared to move to Ramitelli Air Field, home of the 332FG, to which it was assigned.

July 4: The 332FG flew its first mission in the P-51

Lieutenant Colonel Benjamin O. Davis Jr., commanding officer of the 332nd Fighter Group, briefs his crews before a bomber-escort mission.

Mustang aircraft, which replaced the P-47s the group had been flying. The group was assigned to escort B-17s of the 5BW and B-17s of the 47BW, but the rendezvous failed.

July 5: The 332FG escorted Fifteenth Air Force heavy bombers on their way to an enemy target

July 6: The first elements of the 99FS arrived at Ramitelli Airfield, Italy, where the 332FG and its other three squadrons were already based. Although the 99FS had been assigned to the 332FG since May 1, it had flown combat missions while attached to other fighter groups stationed in other parts of Italy. Other squadrons of the 332FG escorted B-24 bombers of the 47BW to Latisana

and Tagilamento-Casarsa, Italy.

July 7: The 332FG failed to rendezvous with bombers it was assigned to escort to Blechhammer, Germany, because the group followed an alternate plan that specified the bombers would be going to Vienna, Austria, instead.

July 8: The 99FS received its first P-51 Mustang aircraft, which was far superior to the P-40s it had flown in the past. Other squadrons of the 332FG escorted B-24 bombers of the 304 BW to, over, and from Muchendorf Airdrome. Enemy fighters were reported to have attacked the escorted bombers. The 332FG mission report number 20 noted "2 B-24s destroyed over target area. 1 B-24 seen to disintegrate, 2 chutes seen to open from 2nd B-24." These bomber losses are not confirmed by Missing Air Crew Reports.

July 9: The 332FG flew its first mission to Ploesti, Romania escorting B-24s of the 47BW on a raid on important petroleum refining facilities.

July 10: Capt Mac Ross of the 99FS was killed in a crash while on a routine transition flight during the squadron's conversion from P-40 to P-51 aircraft.

July 11: The 332FG flew its first mission over occupied France, escorting B-24 bombers of the 47BW to, over, and from Toulon, France, Meanwhile, Capt Leon C. Roberts of the 99FS was killed in a crash on a transition flight as his squadron was converting from P-40 to P-51 aircraft.

July 12: The 332FG escorted the B-24s of the 49th Bomb Wing to raid the marshalling yards at Nimes in southern France and downed four enemy airplanes. 1st Lt Harold E. Sawyer shot down one FW-190 (the first 332FG victory in the P-51 Mustang), while 1st Lt Joseph Elsberry shot down three of them, earning a Distinguished Flying Cross for the achievement. Enemy airplanes shot down at least three of the escorted B-24s, and possibly four.

July 13: The 332FG escorted two B-17 groups of the 5BW to bomb the Pinzano railroad bridge and the Vinzone viaduct in northern Italy.

July 15: The 99FS flew its first combat mission for the Fifteenth Air Force, and its first combat mission with the other three squadrons of the 332FG. This was the second group mission to Ploesti, Romania. The 332FG escorted B-24 bombers of the 55BG, and encountered enemy aircraft, but reported no losses .

July 16: The 332FG conducted a fighter sweep in the Vienna area of Austria. Two Tuskegee Airmen shot down two enemy airplanes. The victors included 1st Lt Alfonza W. Davis and 2nd Lt William W. Green Jr. They each earned a Distinguished Flying Cross for their heroic actions on this date.

July 17: Three members of the 302FS each shot down one Me-109 during a mission to escort B-24s of the 304BW to Avignon, France. The victors included 1st Lts Luther H. Smith Jr., Laurence D. Wilkins and 2nd Lt Robert H. Smith. All of the downed airplanes were ME-109s . For their heroic actions on this date, 1st Lt Luther H. Smith and Laurence D. Wilkins, both of the 302FS, each earned a Distinguished Flying Cross.

July 18: The 332FG escorted B-17s of the 5BW on a raid against an airfield at Memmingen, Germany. Nine Tuskegee Airmen shot down twelve enemy airplanes on this mission in air battles over northeastern Italy and then near the target. 2nd Lt Clarence Lester shot down three Me-109s, and 1st Lt Jack D. Holsclaw shot down two. Other victors included Capt Edward L. Toppins, 1st Lt Charles P. Bailey and Weldon K. Groves, and 2nd Lt Lee A. Archer, Walter J. A. Palmer, Roger Romine, and Hugh S. Warner. Three of the 332FG P-51C pilots, including 2nd Lt Gene

C. Browne and 2nd Lt Wellington G. Irving of the 301FS, were shot down by enemy aircraft near the target area. Lt Browne became a prisoner of war in Germany, but Lt Irving was killed. P-51 pilot Lt Oscar Hutton of the 100FS was also reported lost. Twenty-one of the 332FG's fighters had returned to base after the air battle over northern Italy, leaving only 36 of the group's fighters to escort the bombardment groups of the 5BW. Unfortunately, enemy aircraft shot down 15 of the B-17 bombers in the last two groups of the 5BW to arrive in the Memmingen target area. For their heroism on the Memmingen mission this day, the following five members of the 332FG each earned the Distinguished Flying Cross: 2nd Lt Clarence D. Lester (100FS); 1st Lt Jack D. Holsclaw (100FS); Capt Andrew D. Turner (100FS); 1st Lt Walter J. A. Palmer (100FS); and 1st Lt Charles P. Bailey (99FS). The order awarding Distinguished Flying Crosses to Lts Lester and Holsclaw noted that the bomber formation they guarded was attacked by "300 enemy fighters." Given the very large number of bombers to escort and the very many enemy fighters that attacked them relative to the number of escort fighters, it is understandable that many of the bombers were shot down by enemy aircraft.

July 19: The 332FG escorted B-24 bombers of the 49BW to Munich/Schleiszheim Airdrome

July 20: The 332FG escorted bombers to the Friedrichshafen area of Germany. Four Tuskegee Airmen shot down four Me-109s. The victors included Capts Joseph D. Elsberry, Armour G. McDaniel, and Edward L. Toppins, and 1st Lt Langdon E. Johnson. Elsberry became the first Tuskegee Airman to earn four aerial victory credits. Unfortunately, two of the escorted B-24s were shot down by enemy aircraft. The 332FG

"It has been very dusty in our area" and "We have to find some method to cope with the dust situation here. A good rain would help very much," according to the June 12–13, 1944, war diaries of the 96th Air Service Group at their new base at Foggia, Italy.

flew two air-sea rescue missions over the Adriatic. Capt Henry B. Perry of the 99FS earned the Distinguished Flying Cross for his heroic actions on this date.

July 21: The 332FG escorted B-17 bombers of the 5BW home after they had bombed the Brux synthetic oil refinery in Bohemia (German-held Czechoslovakia). The group reported losing one pilot on the mission, Lt William F. Williams of the 301FS.

July 22: The 332FG escorted B-24 bombers of the 55 BW to and from Ploesti, Romania. 1st Lt James Alonza Walker of the 302FS was reported lost with his P-51C over the Kraljevo area of Yugoslavia, probably as a result of enemy antiaircraft artillery fire. He returned safely on Aug 28 after having evaded enemy forces.

July 24: The 332FG escorted B-24 bombers of the 47BG on a raid to Genoa harbor in northwestern Italy.

July 25: Lt Harold Sawyer of the 301FS shot down one Me-109 German fighter during a mission to escort B-24s of the 55BW to Linz, Austria. For his heroic actions on this date, Capt Sawyer earned the Distinguished Flying Cross. On the same mission, the 301FS reported two of its pilots missing in action, Lts Starling B. Penn and Lt Alfred Q. Carrol.

July 25: 387 Service Group (later 387 Air Service Group) was activated at Daniel Field, Georgia, which ultimately became the "housekeeping" group to support the 477BG. It was composed of primarily black personnel, but the first commander, who served until June 21, 1945, was a white officer, Lt Col David H. Thomas. The 590th Air Materiel Sqn and the 602nd Air Engineering Sqn were eventually assigned to the group.

July 26: Four Tuskegee Airmen each shot down one Me-109 during a mission to escort B-24s of the 47BW to Markendorf Airdrome. The victors included Capt Edward L. Toppins, 1st Lt Freddie E. Hutchins and Leonard M. Jackson, and 2nd Lt Roger Romine. Toppins earned his fourth aerial victory credit. Unfortunately, 2nd Lt Charles S. Jackson Jr. of the 100FS was reported lost with his P-51B after experiencing engine trouble 25 miles northwest of Zagreb, Yugoslavia. He bailed out. He later returned safely, on August 27, after evading enemy forces for more than a month. The 332FG mission report also noted "1 B-24 spiraling out of formation after attack by enemy aircraft," but there is no corresponding Missing Air Crew Report for the bomber.

July 27: The 332FG escorted B-24s of the 47BW raiding an arms factory in the Budapest area of Hungary. North of Lake Balaton they encountered enemy aircraft and six Tuskegee Airmen shot down a total of eight enemy airplanes. 1st Lt Edward C. Gleed and 2nd Lt Alfred M. Gorham each shot down two FW-190s. Other victors, who each shot down one Me-109, included Capt Claude B. Govan, 1st Lt Leonard M. Jackson and Felix J. Kirkpatrick, and 2nd Lt Richard W. Hall. 2nd Lt Emory L. Robbins Jr. of the 302FS was reported missing with his P-51C in the area of the air combat. 1st Lt Edward C. Gleed earned the Distinguished Flying Cross for his heroism on this date.

July 28: The 332FG escorted B-24 bombers of

the 55BW to, over, and from Ploesti, Romania. Three B-24s were seen to go down in flames. The bomber losses are not confirmed by corresponding Missing Air Crew Reports.

July 30: 2nd Lt Carl Johnson shot down an enemy airplane during a mission to escort B-17 bombers of the 5BW to Budapest, Hungary.

July: Members of the 332FG and its squadrons shot down 39 enemy aircraft, more than in any other month of the war.

August: SSgt. Joe Louis, heavyweight boxing champion of the world, visited the 332FG and other groups in Italy, although he did not belong to them.

August 2: The 332FG escorted B-17s of the 5BW to bomb Le Pousin Oil Storage and Portes Le Valences, France. The 332FG mission report (number 42) noted that "Formation of bombers was spread out over area of approximately 50 miles... It was impossible to cover all groups or afford desired protection from E/A (enemy aircraft)."

August 3: The 332FG again escorted B-17 bombers of the 5BW, this time to raid Ober Raderach Chemical Works in Germany. Although four Me-109s were seen in the Udine area on the way, the group reported no encounters and no attacks on the bombers.

August 6: The 332FG escorted B-24 bombers of the 55BW to the Avignon area of southern France. One B-24 was shot down by enemy antiaircraft artillery fire. The 332FG flew a second mission on August 6, this time to escort a single B-25 over Yugoslavia.

August 7: The 332FG escorted B-24s of the 55BW and B-17s of the 5BW to raid enemy oil refineries at Blechhammer. One Me-109 dove through the bombers during the raid. Bombers were shot down, but after the 332FG had finished escorting them.

August 9: The 332FG escorted B-17s of the 5BW on a mission to Gyor, Hungary. 2nd Lt Alphonso Simmons of the 100FS was reported missing with his P-51C about ten miles south of Banja Luka, Yugoslavia. He evaded enemy forces in Yugoslavia for almost a month, returning on Sept 8.

August 10: The 332FG escorted B-24 bombers of the 304BW against the Campina Stevea Romana Oil Refineries.

August 12: The 332FG attacked radar stations in southern France on a strafing mission in preparation for the Allied invasion of southern France (scheduled for August 15). 1st Lt Langdon E. Johnson of the 100FS was seen crashing into the Mediterranean with his P-51C after being hit by flak, in the area ten miles southeast of Marseilles, France. Other 332FG P-51 pilots reported shot down included Lts Alexander Jefferson, Robert Daniels Jr., Richard Macon, and Joseph Gordon. Lts Jefferson, Daniels, and Macon all became prisoners of war in Germany. Lt Gordon did not survive. For their heroic actions on this date, the following six members of the 332FG each earned the Distinguished Flying Cross: Capt Lee Rayford (301FS), Capt Woodrow W. Crockett (100FS), Capt William T. Mattison (100FS), 1st Lt Freddie E. Hutchins (302FS), 1st Lt Lawrence B. Jefferson (301FS), and 1st Lt Lowell C. Steward (100FS).

August 13: The 332FG escorted B-24s of the 304BW on a mission to destroy railroad bridges in the vicinity of Avignon in southern France.

August 14: 2nd Lt George M. Rhodes Jr. of the 100FS shot down one FW-190 German fighter during a strafing and fighter sweep mission in the Toulon area. 2nd Lt Robert O'Neil of the 100FS was last seen in a spin over the Toulon area, and Lt Allen was reported to have bailed out safely over the island of Elba. O'Neil returned on Aug.

26 after having evaded enemy forces in France for almost two weeks. The strafing mission was in preparation for the Allied invasion of southern France. For their heroic actions on this date, the following four members of the 332FG each earned a Distinguished Flying Cross: Capt Melvin T. Jackson (302FS), 1st Lt Gwynne W. Pierson (302FS), Capt Arnold W. Cisco (301FS), and Capt Alton F. Ballard (301FS).

August 14: Back at TAAF, in Alabama, fourteen black officers walked into a section of the post restaurant formerly reserved for white officers and demanded service. They had with them copies of a 1940 War Department directive banning segregation in U.S. Army post exchanges and restaurants. The restaurant manager complied, and Col Noel Parrish, the base commander, agreed that the post restaurant should be integrated.

August 15: The Allies invaded German-occupied southern France, and the 332FG escorted the 55BW to hit targets there. Two Me-109 enemy airplanes were seen, but they did not appear to attack the bomber formation and were too distant for interception. One 332FG pilot, Lt Wilson V. Eagleson, was reported missing.

August 16: The 332FG escorted B-24s of the 55th Bomb Wing on a mission to bomb the Ober Raderach Chemical Works in Germany. P-51C pilot 1st Lt Herbert V. Clark of the 99FS was shot down by enemy antiaircraft artillery over Italy. He survived and returned on May 4, 1945 after evading enemy forces in Italy for more than eight months.

August 17: The 332FG escorted B-24 heavy bombers of the 304BW to, over, and from Ploesti's oil refineries in Romania. Nine bombers were shot down, according to Missing Air Crew Reports, but the reason given was enemy antiaircraft artillery fire.

August 18: The 332FG returned to Ploesti a second day in a row, this time to escort B-17s of the 5BW. No losses were reported.

August 19: The 332FG completed its eighth mission escorting bombers to Ploesti, Romania, and its third in a row to that target. That was its last mission to that target during the war. This time the group escorted B-24 bombers of the 47BW. Lt Thomas was reported to have crash landed on Pianosa Island, but was reported safe.

August 20: The 332FG escorted B-17 heavy bombers of the 5BW to raid the Oswiecim Oil Refinery. The mission encountered some 16 Me-109 and FW-190 German fighter airplanes, but did not report any attack on the bombers.

August 22: The 332FG escorted B-24s of the 55BW to, over, and from the Korneuburg Oil Refineries in Vienna, Austria. They encountered enemy Me-109 fighters over Lake Balaton in Hungary. According to Missing Air Crew Reports, two bombers were lost on the mission, one to enemy antiaircraft artillery and one to an unknown cause. The 332FG flew a second mission, this time to provide escort cover for six C-47s over Yugoslavia. The 96th Air Service Group moved from Foggia to Jesi (Iesi), Italy.

August 23: Flight Officer William L. Hill of the 302FS shot down one Me-109 during a mission to escort B-24 bombers of the 55BW to Markersdorf Airdrome, Germany. Fourteen enemy Me-109 fighters were encountered in the target area. The mission report also noted "1 B-24 seen to go down in flames in T/A (target area)." There was no corresponding Missing Air Crew Report.

August 24: Three Tuskegee Airmen each shot down an enemy aircraft during a mission to escort B-17s of the 5BW to Pardubice Airdrome, Czechoslovakia. The victors included 1st Lt Charles E. McGee and William H. Thomas, who each shot

down a FW-190, and 1st Lt John F. Briggs, who shot down an Me-109. Enemy aircraft shot down one of the escorted B-17 bombers after flak had crippled it and forced it to drop out of the formation. 1st Lt John F. Briggs of the 100FS and 1st Lt William H. Thomas of the 302FS each earned a Distinguished Flying Cross for their heroic actions on this date.

August 25: The 332FG escorted B-17s of the 5BW on a raid against Brno Airdrome. Four enemy Me-109 aircraft were seen on the mission, but there was no apparent aerial combat.

August 26: The 332FG provided close escort to B-24 bombers of the 304BW to Banasea Airdrome. 2nd Lt Henry A. Wise is reported to have bailed out of his P-51 during the mission, and to have landed safely near Krujino, Yugoslavia.

August 27: While returning from a mission to escort B-24s of the 304 and 55BWs to Blechhammer, Germany, units of the 332FG attacked airfields in Czechoslovakia, destroying 22 enemy aircraft on the ground. On the same day, 2Lt Charles S. Jackson returned safely after evading enemy forces in Yugoslavia for more than a month. For heroic actions on this date, the following three members of the 332FG each earned the Distinguished Flying Cross: Capt Wendell O. Pruitt (302FS), Capt Dudley M. Watson (302FS), 1st Lt Roger Romine (302FS).

August 28: The 332FG escorted B-24s of the 47BW against Miskolc Min marshalling yards.

August 29: The 332FG escorted B-17s of the 5BW to Bohumin, Privoser, and Morvaska Main. On the mission, 2nd Lt Emile G. Clifton Jr. of the 99FS bailed out of his P-51B after losing coolant while flying over the area of Zgon, Yugoslavia. Clifton returned on Sept 9, after successfully evading enemy forces in Italy for eleven days.

August 30: The 332FG strafed Grosswardein Airdrome in Romania and claimed to have destroyed 83 enemy aircraft on the ground. 2nd Lt Charles T. Williams of the 301FS was reported lost with his P-51 over Yugoslavia during the mission. He became a prisoner of war. Capt Clarence H. Bradford of the 301FS earned the Distinguished Flying Cross for his heroic actions on this date.

August 31: The 366th and 367th Service Squadrons at Ramitelli and Vasta were redesignated as the 366th and 367th Air Service Squadrons. They were still assigned to the 96th Air Service Group, headquartered in Foggia.

August 31 and September 1: The 332FG, along with five other fighter groups of the Fifteenth Air Force, escorted more than 50 B-17s bombers of the 5BW's 2 and 97BGs that flew to Romania's Popesti Airdrome to carry more than 1,000 American airmen who had been held as prisoners of war from Romania to Italy. Operation Reunion, as it was called, involved B-17s that had been modified to carry up to 20 personnel each in their bomb bays.

September 1: Maj George S. Roberts replaced Capt Erwin B. Lawrence Jr. as commander of the 99FS. Maj Roberts had commanded the squadron twice previously, and had been the first black commander of the squadron.

September 2: The 332FG conducted a strafing mission to Stalac, Cuprija, and Osipaonica Road in Yugoslavia.

September 3: The 332FG escorted B-24 bombers of the 304BW to Szolnok and Szeged, Hungary. Brig Gen Yantis H. Taylor replaced Brig Gen Dean C. Strother as commander of the 306th FW, under which had served the seven fighter squadrons (six white and one black) of the XV Fighter Command of the Fifteenth Air Force. Strother also became commander of the new XV Fighter Command. The Fifteenth Air Force

organized a provisional 305FW, which assumed management of the three P-38 groups, while the 306th FW retained direct control of the four P-51 fighter groups, including the 332nd.

September 4: The 332FG escorted B-24 bombers of the 304BW again, this time to Tagliamento Casarsa and Latisana, Italy.

September 5: The 332FG escorted B-17s of the 5BW to Budapest, Hungary, and back.

September 6: The 332FG escorted B-17s of the 5BW for a second day, but this time to the Oradea Main marshalling yards in Romania.

September 7: The 67th AAF Base Unit was organized at Tuskegee (Tuskegee Weather Detachment).

September 8: The 332FG claimed to have destroyed 36 enemy airplanes on the ground at two airfields during a strafing mission to Yugoslavia. P-51 pilot Lt James A. Calhoun crashed and was killed in the target area. Maj George S. Roberts of the 332FG and 1st Lt Heber C. Houston of the 99FS each earned a Distinguished Flying Cross for his heroic actions on this date.

September 10: Lt Gen Ira C. Eaker, commander of the Mediterranean Allied Air Force; Maj Gen Nathan F. Twining, commander of the Fifteenth Air Force; Brig Gen Dean C. Strother, commander of the XV Fighter Command; and Brig Gen Benjamin O. Davis Sr., Inspector General's Department, attended an impressive awards ceremony for members of the 332FG at Ramitelli Airfield, Italy. At that ceremony, Gen Davis presented the Distinguished Flying Cross to his son, Col Benjamin O. Davis Jr., commander of the group, for an escort mission he led on June 9. Capt Joseph D. Elsberry, Lt Jack D. Holsclaw, and Lt Clarence D. "Lucky" Lester were also awarded Distinguished Flying Crosses in the ceremony.

September 12: The 332FG escorted B-17 bomb-

Major General Nathan F. Twining presenting award to a 332nd Fighter Group pilot.

ers of the 5BW on a mission to an unspecified target. The group mission report states "10 Me 109s attacked rear of bomber formation from below...1 B-17 was left burning. 6 chutes seen to open." The 301 and 463BGs of the 5BW each reported a bomber lost. Missing Air Crew Reports do not confirm these bombers were lost to enemy aircraft. Members of the 332FG claimed to have damaged four enemy aircraft during the mission.

September 13: The 332FG escorted B-24 and B-17 bombers of the 304 and 5BWs to Blechhammer North Oil Refinery. The mission report notes "Two B-24s hit by flak seen to explode and crash. No chutes seen." Lt Wilbur Long and his P-51 were reported missing near Szombathely. Lt Long became a prisoner of war in Germany.

September 17: The 332FG escorted B-17s of the 5BW to raid the Rakos marshalling yards of north Budapest, Hungary.

September 18: The 332FG escorted B-24 bombers of the 304BW to raid the Shell Oil Refinery and railroad bridges in Budapest, Hungary. The group reported seeing a B-24 hit by flak in the target area, and seven men parachuting from it.

September 20: The 332FG escorted B-24s of the 304BW again, this time to attack the Makacky Airdrome in Czechoslovakia.

September 21: The 332FG escorted B-17 bombers of the 5BW to raid the Debreczen Marshalling Yards in Hungary.

September 22: The 332FG escorted B-17 bombers of the 5th BW to hit the Allach BMW Engine Works in Munich, Germany. Flight Officer Leonard R. Willette of the 99FS and his P-51 were reported lost near Lake Chien, Germany

September 23: The 332FG escorted B-17s of the 5BW to bomb the Brux synthetic oil plant.

September 24: The 332FG escorted B-24 bombers of the 304BW as they raided enemy targets in Athens, Greece.

October 4: The 332FG took part in three missions, two to escort C-47 transport aircraft to Sofia, Bulgaria and Bucharest, Romania, and one to strafe targets in Tatoi, Kalamaki, and Eleusis, Greece. In Greece, the group reported destroying nine enemy aircraft on the ground. Capts Erwin B. Lawrence and Kenneth I. Williams, both of the 99FS, were reported lost or missing in the Athens area. For their heroic actions on this date, the following five members of the 332FG each earned the Distinguished Flying Cross: 1st Lt Samuel L. Curtis (100FS), 1st Lt Dempsey Morgan (100FS), Capt Claude B. Govan (301FS), 1st Lt Herman A. Lawson (99FS), and 1st Lt Willard L. Woods (100FS).

October 6: The 332FG strafed enemy airdromes in

Tatoi, Kalamaki, Eleusis, and Megara in Greece, similar to the mission two days earlier. This was in preparation for the Allied invasion of Greece. Four 332FG pilots were reported missing on this mission, including 1st Lt Freddie E. Hutchins of the 302FS, who was seen to crash about three miles west of Megara after the explosion of an ammunition dump; 1st Lt Carroll S. Woods of the 100FS, whose P-51 was seen flaming in the area of Kalamaki Airdrome; 2nd Lt Joe A. Lewis of the 301FS, who was seen to crash near Athens after being hit by antiaircraft artillery fire; and 2nd Lt Andrew D. Marshall of the 301FS. Marshall returned on October 14 after evading enemy forces in Greece for eight days. Hutchins also returned from Greece, but not until October 25. For their heroic actions on this date, the following five members of the 332FG each earned a Distinguished Flying Cross: 1st Lt Alva N. Temple (99FS), Capt Lawrence E. Dickson (100FS), 1st Lt Edward M. Thomas (99FS), 1st Lt Robert L. Martin (100FS), and Capt Robert J. Friend (301FS).

October 7: The 332FG returned to escorting bombers, this time protecting B-17s of the 5BW on a raid against the Lobau Oil Refineries at Vienna, Austria. Lt Robert Wiggins, 2nd Lt Roosevelt Stiger of the 302FS and Flight Officer Carl J. Woods of the 100FS were reported lost on this mission. Stiger and Woods were last seen over the Adriatic Sea. One B-17 was reported hit at 30,000 feet, but there is no corresponding Missing Air Crew Report.

October 11: The 332FG strafed railroad and river traffic along the Danube River from Budapest to Bratislava, and reported destroying 17 enemy airplanes on the ground. Lt Rhodes was reported to have crash landed at Ramitelli. The airplane was destroyed, but the pilot survived. Capt Wil-

liam A. Campbell, 1st Lt George E. Gray, and 1st Lt Richard S. Harder of the 99FS and 1st Lt Felix J. Kirkpatrick of the 302FS, each earned a Distinguished Flying Cross for his heroic actions on this day.

October 12: The 332FG strafed railroad traffic from Budapest to Bratislava for a second day in a row. Six members of the 332FG's 302FS shot down a total of nine enemy airplanes. 1 Lt Lee Archer shot down three Me-109s, bringing his total aerial victories score to four. Capt Wendell O. Pruitt shot down two enemy airplanes, including an He-111 and an Me-109. Other victors included Capt Milton R. Brooks, 1st Lt William W. Green Jr, Roger Romine, and Luther H. Smith Jr. Enemy antiaircraft artillery shot down 1st Lt Walter L. McCreary of the 100FS about 25 miles southeast of Lake Balaton, Hungary, at approximately 2 p.m. For their heroic actions on this day, the following nine pilots of the 332FG each earned the Distinguished Flying Cross: 1st Lt Lee Archer (302FS), Capt Milton R. Brooks (302FS), 1st Lt Frank E. Roberts (100FS), 1st Lt Spurgeon N. Ellington (100FS), 1st Lt Leonard F. Turner (301FS), Capt Armour G. McDaniel (301FS), Capt Stanley L. Harris (301FS), 1st Lt Marion R. Rodgers (99FS), and 1st Lt Quitman C. Walker (99FS).

October 13: The 332FG resumed bomber escort duty, protecting B-24s of the 304BW to, over, and from Blechhammer South Oil Refinery. On the mission the group reported having destroyed seven enemy airplanes on the ground. Enemy antiaircraft artillery fire shot down three of the 332FG pilots, all of whom belonged to the 302FS. They were 1st Lts Walter D. Westmoreland, William W. Green Jr., and Luther H. Smith Jr. Westmoreland was seen to crash in Hungary, and Smith was seen to parachute over Yugoslavia. Lt

Smith was injured trying to abandon his burning P-51, and was captured. Green disappeared over Yugoslavia. One B-24 was also seen to crash, probably also as result of flak. 1st Lt Milton S. Hays of the 99FS earned a Distinguished Flying Cross for his heroic actions on this day.

October 14: The 332FG escorted B-24s of the 49BW on a raid against the Odertal Oil Refineries in Germany. Flight Officer Rual W. Bell of the 100FS was seen to parachute out of his P-51C after engine trouble over Yugoslavia. Bell returned on October 23 after having evaded enemy forces in Yugoslavia for nine days. 1st Lt George M. Rhodes Jr. of the 100FS earned a Distinguished Flying Cross for his heroic actions on this day.

October 16: The 332FG escorted B-17s of the 5BW to bomb the Brux oil refineries.

October 17: The 332FG conducted two missions, one to escort B-17s of the 5BW to the Blechhammer South Oil Refinery, and one to escort a single B-17 of the same wing to Bucharest, Romania.

October 20: The 332FG conducted two missions, one to escort B-17s of the 5BW to raid the Brux Oil Refineries (target cover and withdrawal) and one air-sea rescue escort to Rimini to protect a Catalina search and rescue aircraft. Capt Alfonza W. Davis assumed command of the 99FS.

October 21: The 332FG flew its 100th mission for the Fifteenth Air Force. It escorted B-24s of the 304BW to, over, and from Gyor, Hungary. The 332FG flew its 101st mission, this one a search of the Venezia area. Capt Vernon V. Haywood of the 302FS earned the Distinguished Flying Cross for his heroic actions on this day.

October 23: The 332FG escorted B-24 bombers of the 304BW to Regensburg and back. 1st Lts Robert C. Chandler and Shelby F. Westbrook, both of the 99FS, were reported missing with their P-51Cs. Chandler survived a crash, and eventu-

ally returned. Westbrook also returned, a month after he was reported Missing in Action, having evaded enemy forces in Yugoslavia.

October 29: The 332FG flew four missions. One escorted B-24 bombers of the 49BW to and from Regensburg. Two members of the 332FG, Capt Alfonza W. Davis of the 99FS in a P-51D, and 2nd Lt Fred L. Brewer Jr. of the 100FS in a *, were reported missing, Davis over the Gulf of Trieste and Brewer over Germany. Two other October 29 mission reports each noted that the group escorted a P-38 for reconnaissance of the Munich area. Finally, a fourth mission report for the day noted that the 332FG escorted two B-25s on a mission to Bredgrad and Glina, Yugoslavia. Maj William A. Campbell assumed command of the 99FS.

November 1: The 332FG reported flying three missions, one to escort two B-25s to Yugoslavia, one to escort B-24 bombers of the 304BW to Vienna, Austria, and back, and one to escort one C-47 transport aircraft to Yugoslavia.

November 2: The 302FS emblem was approved. On a disk, it depicted a winged running red devil with a machine gun, over a cloud.

November 3: Maj George S. Roberts became commander of the 332FG, temporarily replacing Col Benjamin O. Davis Jr., who returned to command the group on December 24.

November 4: The 332FG escorted B-17 bombers of the 5BW to Regensburg, Germany. The 332FG also flew two reconnaissance escort missions, each to escort a lone P-38, one over the Linz area of Austria and one over the Munich area of Germany.

November 5: The 332FG flew three missions again in one day. One escorted B-17s of the 5BW to and from Florisdorf, Austria, and two others each to escort a single P-38 reconnaissance aircraft over the Munich area.

November 6: The 332FG escorted B-17s of the 5BW to and from Mossbierbaum oil refinery in the Vienna area of Austria. Capt William J. Faulkner Jr. of the 301FS was reported missing over Austria on that mission, possibly because of mechanical failure of his P-51C.

November 7: The 332FG provided target cover for B-24s of the 55BW raiding the Trento and Bolzano areas of northern Italy.

November 11: The 332FG escorted B-17s of the 5BW to and over the Brux oil refineries. At least one of the group pilots reported seeing a jet-propelled aircraft in the distance. Lt Payne crash landed at Lesina. The airplane was destroyed, but he survived, while 2nd. Lt Elton H. Nightingale of the 301FS was reported missing over Italy with his P-51B.

November 16: The 332FG escorted B-24 bombers of the 304BW to and from Munich West marshalling yards. During the mission, the group encountered several Me-109s that attempted to shoot down the bombers. Capt Luke J. Weathers of the 302FS shot down two of the enemy fighters. The 52FG also escorted the 304BW. For his heroic actions following a take-off accident, Capt Woodrow W. Crockett of the 100FS was awarded the Soldiers Medal. After two P-51s crashed into each other and caught fire, Capt Crockett, at the risk of his own life, entered the burning wreckage to aid the trapped pilots. He was able to rescue one of them, Lt William Hill, before the burning planes exploded. Unfortunately, Lt Roger Romine died in the accident. Capt Luke J. Weathers of the 302FS earned the Distinguished Flying Cross for his heroic actions on this day.

November 17: The 332FG escorted B-17s of the 5BW back to Brux synthetic oil refinery.

November 18: The 332FG escorted heavy bombers raiding the Vicenza-Villafranca area of northern Italy. Lt Peoples was reported missing.

November 19: The 332FG conducted a strafing mission against enemy railway, highway, and river traffic targets in the Gyor-Vienna-Esztergom area of Austria. 1st Lt Roger B. Gaiter of the 99FS was seen to bail out of his P-51 after it was hit by enemy antiaircraft fire. 1st Lt Quitman Walker, also of the 99FS, was reported missing after being hit by flak. Both were lost near Lake Balaton, Hungary. For this mission, the Fifteenth Air Force commander Maj Gen Nathan F. Twining commended the 332FG. For their heroic actions on this day, the following four members of the 332FG each earned the Distinguished Flying Cross: Capt Albert H. Manning (99FS), Capt John Daniels (99FS), 1st Lt William N. Alsbrook (99FS), and 1st Lt Norman W. Scales (100FS).

November 20: The 332FG escorted B-17 bombers of the 5BW to and from Blechhammer South oil refinery. The group also escorted B-24s of the 55BW to the same target. 1st Lt Maceo A. Harris Jr. of the 100FS was reported missing after his P-51C lost coolant over Germany.

November 20: Eugene G. Theodore of Trinidad became the last foreign cadet to graduate from pilot training at TAAF.

November 22: 332FG fighters escorted two B-25 medium bombers to and from Pedgrad, Yugoslavia.

November 25: The 100FS emblem was approved. It depicted, on a disk, a winged panther on a globe.

November 26: 332FG P-51s escorted one reconnaissance P-38 aircraft to and from Grodenwoh and Nurnberg, Germany.

December: At least by the end of the week ending on December 2, the 366th Air Service Squadron at Ramitelli Airfield in Italy began issuing

110-gallon auxiliary fuel tanks to the 332FG. The 332FG had been using smaller 75-gallon wing tanks. The larger fuel tanks, also attached to the wings of the P-51 airplanes, allowed them to fly on longer missions, such as the famous one to Berlin almost four months later (March 24).

December 2: The 332FG escorted B-24s of the 49 and 55BWs on a raid to Blechhammer oil refinery (South). Lt Cornelius P. Gould Jr. of the 301FS was reported to have bailed safely out of his P-51B after experiencing engine trouble over Czechoslovakia.

December 3: The 332FG escorted B-24 bombers of the 49BW to and from the Udine Pass area of northern Italy. Lt Marion R. Rodgers was reported to have crash-landed safely at Ramitelli Air Base, home base of the 332nd.

December 9: The 332FG escorted B-17s of the 5BW to Brux, Germany. For the first time, they encountered some German Me-262 jet aircraft. Lt Rich and Lt Brown were reported missing.

December 11: The 332FG flew two missions, one to escort B-24s of the 47BW to and from the Moosbierbaum oil refinery of Austria, and one to escort a reconnaissance aircraft to Praha, Czechoslovakia. On the Moosbierbaum mission, one B-24 was seen to explode in the Vienna area.

December 15: The 332FG escorted B-24s of the 47BW to and from Innsbruck, Austria.

December 16: The 332FG flew two missions, one to escort B-17s of the 5BW to and from Brux, Germany, and one to escort a single B-25 to Mrkoplj, Yugoslavia.

December 17: The 332FG escorted B-17s of the 5BW and B-24s of the 49 and 304BWs on withdrawal from a raid on Olomouc (Olmutz), Germany.

December 18: The 332FG flew two missions, one to escort B-24 Liberators of the 49BW to and from oil refineries at Blechhammer, and one to escort a P-38 on a reconnaissance mission to Innsbruck, Austria.

December 19: The 332FG again flew two missions, one to escort B-24s of the 55BW to and from Blechhammer South oil refinery, and one to escort a P-38 on a reconnaissance mission to Praha (Prague), Czechoslovakia.

December 20: The 332FG flew two missions, one to escort B-17 Flying Fortresses of the 5BW to and from an oil refinery at Brux, and one to escort a single P-38 on a reconnaissance mission to Prague, Czechoslovakia.

December 22: After a day without a mission, the 332FG escorted one P-38 on a reconnaissance mission to and from Ingolstadt, Germany.

December 23: The 332FG again escorted a single P-38 on a reconnaissance mission, this time to Praha (Prague), Czechoslovakia. Capt Lawrence E. Dickson of the 100FS was reported to have bailed out of his P-51D over Italy because of engine trouble.

December 24: Col Benjamin O. Davis Jr. resumed command of the 332FG, replacing Maj George S. Roberts, who had commanded the group since November 3.

December 25: After a day without a mission, the 332FG escorted Fifteenth Air Force Bombers (number and wing not specified) during a raid on the Brux oil refinery, Germany. Although no enemy aircraft were encountered, Me-109 German fighters were seen chasing B-26 medium bombers in the distance.

December 26: The 332FG escorted B-17s of the 5BW and B-24s of the 55BW on withdrawal from the Odertal and Blechhammer oil refineries of Germany.

December 27: The 332FG escorted B-17s Flying

Fortresses of the 5BW to and from oil refineries in the Vienna area of Austria. During the mission, a B-17 was seen to explode in the Linz area.

December 28: The 332FG escorted B-24s of the 304BW to and from the Kolin and Pardubice oil refineries in Czechoslovakia.

December 29: For the second day in a row, the 332FG escorted B-24s of the 304BW, this time to and from targets in Muhldorf and Lanshut, Germany. At noon, 1st Lt Frederick D. Funderburg Jr. and 2nd Lt Andrew D. Marshall, both of the 301FS, were reported missing with their P-51Cs over the Munich area of Germany. Lts Robert J. Friend and Lewis Craig were reported to have bailed out of their P-51s. Bad weather forced many Fifteenth Air Force B-24 crews returning from their mission to land their bombers at alternative fields. Eighteen of the Liberators, 17 from the 485BG and one from the 455BG, landed at Ramitelli Air Field, Italy, the home base of the 332FG, where the bomber crews spent five days enjoying the hospitality of the Tuskegee Airmen.

1945

January 1: Brig Gen Dean C. Strother, commander of the XV Fighter Command, awarded Distinguished Flying Crosses to seven 332FG pilots, including Maj Lee Rayford and Capts Andrew D. Turner, William A. Campbell, Melvin T. Jackson, Vernon Haywood, Dudley Watson, and George E. Gray.

January 3: 332FG pilot strength was noted as 121, with overall personnel numbering 1250. After four days without missions, the 332FG provided reconnaissance escort for a P-38 to the Munich and Linz areas of Germany and Austria.

January 5: The 332FG escorted one Mosquito aircraft on a reconnaissance mission to the Munich area of Germany.

January 8: After two days without missions, the 332FG escorted B-24 Liberators of the 47BW to and from the marshalling yards of Linz, Austria.

January 11: The 387th Air Service Group moved from Daniel Field, Georgia, to Godman Field, Kentucky, where it was welcomed by Col Robert R. Selway Jr., commander of Godman Field. According to the group history, "Recreational facilities at Godman were adequate to satisfy most of the men" under Col Selway, who was also commander of the 477 BG.

January 15: After six days without missions, the 332FG escorted B-24s of the 304BW to and from a raid on targets in Vienna, Austria.

January 18: After two days without a mission, the 332FG flew two missions, each to escort a single P-38 for reconnaissance photographs over Germany. One went to Stuttgart and the other went to Munich.

January 19: Six P-51s of the 332FG escorted a single P-38 to Praha (Prague), Czechoslovakia for reconnaissance photographs. The P-38 suffered engine failure and the pilot had to bail out. One of the six escorts landed at a field other than Ramitelli.

January 20: The 332FG flew two missions, one that escorted B-17 Flying Fortresses of the 5BW to oil storage targets at Regensburg, Germany, and one that escorted a single P-38 on a photographic reconnaissance mission to and from Praha (Prague), Czechoslovakia. On the latter mission, the escort formation ran into a snowstorm and became separated. The 96th Service Group was officially redesignated as the 96th Air Service Group.

January 21: The 332FG escorted B-17s of the 5BW

for a second day in a row, but this time to and from Vienna Lobau Distillation Unit and Schwechat Oil Refinery. Two German fighter jet Me-262s were seen following the bomber formation. According to Missing Air Crew Reports, three of the bombers were lost, two because of mechanical difficulty, and one to an unknown cause. Two of the 332FG P-51 pilots, both from the 100FS, were also reported lost, both because of engine trouble. Flight Officer Samuel J. Foreman was reported missing over northern Yugoslavia at 1100 hours, and 2nd Lt Albert L. Young was reported missing at 1205 near Vienna, Austria. A Lt Smith was hit by enemy antiaircraft artillery at Wiener Neustadt.

January 22: Col Benjamin O. Davis Jr., commander of the 332FG, presented Distinguished Flying Crosses to 11 332FG pilots, including Maj George S. Roberts, Capts Woodrow W. Crockett, Samuel L. Curtis, Claude B. Govan, Freddie Hutchins, William T. Mattison, Gwynne W. Pierson, Lowell C. Steward, Alva N. Temple, Luke J. Weathers Jr., and 1st Lt Frank Roberts.

January 31: After nine days without missions, because of bad winter weather that obscured targets, the 332FG escorted B-24s of the 47th and 55BWs to and from the Moosbierbaum Oil Refinery in the Vienna area of Austria.

February 1: The 332FG flew two different missions, one to escort B-24s of the 49BW and one to escort B-24s of the 47BW, but both wings with their escorts raided the same target: Moobierbaum Oil Refinery in the Vienna area of Austria

.

February 3: P-51 fighter pilots of the 332FG escorted a single P-38 on a photographic reconnaissance mission over the Munich area of southern Germany.

February 5: The 332FG escorted B-24 Liberators of the 47BW to and from the marshalling yards and main railroad station at Salzburg, Austria.

February 6: The 332FG conducted a fighter sweep over Yugoslavia.

February 7: The 332FG flew two different missions, one to escort B-24s of the 47BW and one to escort B-24s of the 304BW, but both wings raided the same target: Moosbierbaum Oil Refinery in the Vienna area of Austria . The two missions were similar to those on February 1.

February 8: The 332FG flew three missions. On one of the missions, P-51 fighters escorted a single P-38 aircraft on a photographic reconnaissance mission over Stuttgart, Germany. On a second mission, 332FG pilots conducted a fighter sweep over Yugoslavia. On the third mission of the day, the 332FG escorted B-24 bombers of the 55BW to and from Vienna South depots in Austria.

February 11: 2nd Lt Thomas C. Street of the 99FS died while serving overseas.

February 12: P-51 fighter pilots of the 332FG escorted a single P-38 airplane on a photographic reconnaissance mission to and from Praha (Prague), Czechoslovakia.

February 13: The 332FG flew three missions. On one mission, the group escorted a P-38 aircraft on a reconnaissance mission over Munich in southern Germany. On the second mission, the group escorted B-24 Liberators of the 49BW to and from Vienna Central railroad repair shops in Austria. On its third mission the 332FG escorted bombers over Zagreb, Maribor, and Graz. A pilot reported seeing an unidentified jet-propelled enemy aircraft in the distance. One of the 332FG pilots also reported hearing a radio transmission from a bomber noting a jet-propelled aircraft had made a pass at the bombers.

February 14: The 332FG flew two missions, one to escort B-17 Flying Fortresses of the 5BW, and one to escort B-24 Liberators of the 55BW, but both wings attacked the same targets: oil refineries in Vienna, Lobau, and Schwechat. On both missions, the 332FG provided penetration, target cover, and withdrawal escort for the bombers.

February 15: The 332FG flew two missions to escort two different sections of the B-24s of the 49BW (Red Force and Blue Force) to and from the Penzinger marshalling yards in Vienna, Austria.

February 16: The 332FG flew three missions. The group escorted a Mosquito aircraft on a photographic reconnaissance mission over Munich and a P-38 aircraft on another photographic reconnaissance mission over Munich. On the third mission P-51 pilots of the 332FG escorted B-17 Flying Fortresses of the 5BW to and from the airdrome at Lechfeld, Germany. On this mission, 2nd Lt John M. Chavis of the 99FS was reported lost with his P-51C at 1020 hours over Italy. On this mission, 332FG pilots reported seeing three bombers explode in the air, including two B-17s near Bolzano, Italy, and a B-24 (not assigned to the 332FG for escort) near Innsbruck, Austria. Capt Emile G. Clifton of the 99FS earned a Distinguished Flying Cross for his heroic actions on this day.

February 17: The 332FG flew three missions in one day, again. The group escorted a P-38 on a reconnaissance mission to Nurnberg, Germany. The group also escorted a Mosquito aircraft on another reconnaissance mission, this one to Munich, Germany. A pilot reported seeing jet aircraft in the distance on this mission. On its third mission of the day, the group strafed railroad targets between Linz and Vienna, Austria. Capt Louis G. Purnell of the 301FS earned the Distinguished Flying Cross for his heroic actions

on this day.

February 18: The 332FG flew two missions, one to escort B-24 bombers of the 47BW to and from the Wels marshalling yards in the Linz area of Austria, and one to escort a single P-38 aircraft on a photographic reconnaissance mission in the Linz area.

February 19: The 332FG escorted B-24 Liberator bombers of the 49BW to and from the Vienna area of Austria. A Spitfire with British markings was seen firing on the formation.

A bombardment group ground crewmember prepares to load a bomb on an aircraft's bomb rack. The ground crew made sure their pilots had the best advantage possible for missions against the enemy.

February 20: The 332FG flew two missions, one to escort a single P-38 aircraft on a photographic reconnaissance mission over Nurnberg, Germany, and another to escort B-24s of the 47BW to and from Vipitento and Brenner marshalling yards. The second mission report for the day noted that the "fighters had to leave bombers because of shortage of gas".

February 21: The 332FG escorted B-24 Liberators of the 304BW on a raid to Vienna's central marshalling yards.

February 22: The 332FG flew three missions. The group escorted B-17 Flying Fortresses of the 5BW to provide target cover during raids on marshalling yards in southeastern Germany. The other two missions escorted P-38s on photographic reconnaissance missions, one to Prague, Czechoslovakia and Linz, Austria, and one to Stuttgart, Germany.

February 23: The 332FG escorted B-24 Liberator bombers of the 304BW to Gmund West marshalling yards in Germany.

February 24: P-51 fighter pilots of the 332FG escorted a Mosquito aircraft on a photographic reconnaissance mission over the Munich area of southern Germany.

February 25: The 332FG flew two missions, one to strafe railroad traffic in southern Germany and Austria, and one to escort a single P-38 aircraft on a photographic reconnaissance mission over the Munich area. Three of the 332FG P-51C pilots were reported missing. 1st Lt Alfred M. Gorham of the 301FS was reported lost at 1145 hours east of Munich after experiencing mechanical failure. 2nd Lt Wendell W. Hockaday of the 99FS was reported missing at 1225 over Uttendorf, Austria, after suffering damage during a strafing attack. 2nd Lt George J. Iles, also of the 99FS, was reported missing at 1245 hours

over Augsburg, Germany, after being hit by antiaircraft artillery fire. 1st Lts Roscoe C. Brown and Reid E. Thompson, both of the 100FS, each earned the Distinguished Flying Cross for his heroism on this day.

February 26: P-51 fighters of the 332FG escorted a Mosquito aircraft on a photographic reconnaissance mission over Munich in southern Germany.

February 27: The 332FG escorted B-24s of the 49BW to and from the Augsburg marshalling yards in Germany. No enemy aircraft were encountered, but at least one pilot saw what he believed to be a German Me-163 in the distance.

February 28: The 332FG flew three missions, two of them to escort P-38 airplanes on two separate photographic missions over Praha (Prague), Czechoslovakia, and one to escort B-17 Flying Fortresses of the 5BW over Verona in northern Italy. The third mission of the day was the 200th mission of the 332FG for the Fifteenth Air Force. Of those 200 missions, 138 had been to escort bombers.

March 1: The 332FG flew four missions. One escorted a P-38 airplane on a photographic reconnaissance mission over Praha (Prague), Czechoslovakia, and two escorted P-38s on photographic reconnaissance missions over Stuttgart, Germany. The fourth mission escorted B-24 Liberator bombers of the 55BW to and from the Moobierbaum oil refineries in the Vienna area of Austria.

March 2: The 332FG flew two missions, one to escort a single P-38 on a photographic reconnaissance mission over Praha (Prague), Czechoslovakia, and the the other to escort B-24 bombers of the 304BW to, over, and from the marshalling yards of Linz, Austria.

March 2-7: The squadrons (616th, 617th, 618th,

and 619th) of the 477BG moved to Freeman Field, Indiana.

March 3: The 332FG conducted a strafing mission against railroad targets between Maribor, Bruck, and Weiner-Neustadt. 1st Lts Robert L. Martin and Alphonso Simmons, both P-51D pilots of the 100FS, were reported missing on that mission after having been hit by antiaircraft artillery fire at 1410 hours over Graz Airdrome, Austria. Simmons had been reported Missing in Action before, in August 1944, but had returned in September of that year. Martin later returned after his March 3, 1945 loss, after evading enemy forces in Yugoslavia for more than a month.

March 4: The 332FG flew two missions, one to escort B-24s of the 49BW to, over, and from the marshalling yards of Graz. On that mission, one B-24 was seen going down, with six crew members parachuting out of the bomber. On the other mission, P-51 fighter pilots of the 332FG escorted a Mosquito type aircraft on a photographic reconnaissance mission over Munich in southern Germany.

March 5: The 477BG moved from Godman Field, Kentucky, to Freeman Field, Indiana, a larger base which had recently been vacated as a twin-engine pilot training station. The squadrons assigned to the group moved to the same base between March 2 and 7.

March 6: 332FG pilots escorted a P-38 on a photographic reconnaissance mission over the Klagenfurt and Linz areas of Austria. The 302FS was inactivated, leaving the 332FG with three fighters squadrons, the 99th, 100th, and 301st. From then until the end of the war, the 332FG had the same number of fighter squadrons as the other six fighter groups of the Fifteenth Air Force.

March 7: The 332FG again escorted a P-38 on a photographic reconnaissance mission, this time over Munich, Germany.

March 7: The 387th Air Service Group moved from Godman Field, Kentucky, to Freeman Field, Indiana, to which the 477BG, which the 387th Air Service Group supported, had already moved two days earlier.

March 9: The 332FG flew three missions in one day. Two of them escorted P-38s on photographic reconnaissance missions, one to Linz, Austria, and one to the Munich area of Germany. The third mission escorted B-17 Flying Fortress bombers of

A Tuskegee Airman, one of the sergeants in a support personnel role, takes a break on his cot to read a letter from home.

the 5BW to, over, and from the marshalling yards at Bruck, Austria.

March 9: Mr. Truman K. Gibson, civilian aide to the Secretary of War (Henry I. Stimson) visited the 332FG at Ramitelli Air Field, accompanied by Maj Gen James M. Bevans, deputy commander of the Mediterranean Allied Air Forces. The visit reflected the War Department's interest in the success of the group.

March 10: An article by Roi Ottley entitled "Dark Angels of Doom" was published in *Liberty Magazine*. It suggested that members of the 332FG had never lost a bomber in more than 100 missions, despite the fact some of the group's escorted bombers were shot down by enemy aircraft the previous summer.

March 12: The 332FG, after not flying missions for two days, flew three missions, as it had on March 9. Two escorted P-38s on photographic reconnaissance missions, one to the Linz area of Austria and one to Munich, Germany. The third mission escorted B-24s of the 47BW to, over, and from the Floridsdorf oil refinery in the Vienna area of Austria. During the mission, pilots reported having heard on the radio that an aircraft was being jumped by enemy aircraft. Capt Walter M. Downs of the 301FS earned the Distinguished Flying Cross for his heroic actions on this date.

March 13: The 332FG again flew three missions. Two escorted P-38s on photographic reconnaissance missions, one to Stuttgart, Germany, and the other to Nurnberg, Germany. The third mission escorted B-17 Flying Fortress bombers to, over, and from the marshalling yards at Regensburg, Germany. On two of the missions, enemy FW-190 fighter airplanes were seen. On the bomber escort mission, the bombers were early and the fighters were late to the rendezvous point.

March 14: The 332FG flew four missions. One strafed targets on the railroad line connecting Bruck, Leoben, and Steyr. One escorted B-24s of the 47BG to, over, and from a railroad bridge and marshalling yards at Varazdin, Yugoslavia. The other two missions escorted P-38 airplanes on photographic reconnaissance missions over Munich. On one of those missions, at least one pilot reported seeing a German Me-262 jet in the distance. 1st Lt Harold H. Brown of the 99FS was reported lost with his P-51C at 1115 hours east of Bruck, Austria, after being damaged during a strafing attack. For their heroic actions on this day, the following five members of the 332FG and its 99FS each earned a Distinguished Flying Cross: 1st Lt Shelby F. Westbrook, 1st Lt Hannibal M. Cox, 2nd Lt Vincent I. Mitchell, 1st Lt Thomas P. Braswell, and 2nd Lt John W. Davis.

March 15: The 332FG flew two missions, one to provide target cover for Fifteenth Air Force B-24s on raids in the area from Flotsam to Geisha, Yugoslavia, and one to escort B-17s of the 5BW to Zittau, Germany.

March 16: Lt William S. Price III of the 301FS shot down an Me-109 during a strafing mission against railroad targets. This was the first day in four months that members of the 332FG shot down enemy aircraft, reflecting the diminished enemy aircraft opposition during the winter. One 332FG P-51B pilot, 1st Lt Jimmie D. Wheeler of the 99FS, was lost with his P-51B at 1320 hours over Muhldorf, Germany, after he struck a tree on the strafing mission. There were three other missions that day. Two escorted Mosquito type aircraft on photographic reconnaissance missions, one over Munich, Germany, and the other over Prague, Czechoslovakia. The fourth mission escorted Fifteenth Air Force B-24s over and from Monfalcone Harbor, Italy. 1st Lt Roland W. Moody, Henry R. Peoples, and William S. Price III, all of the 301FS, each earned the Distinguished Flying Cross for their heroic actions on this day.

March 17: The 332FG flew two missions to escort P-38s on photographic reconnaissance missions, one to Prague, Czechoslovakia, and the other to Linz, Austria.

March 19: The 332FG flew three missions, two to escort Mosquito type aircraft on photographic missions, one to the Linz and Munich areas of Austria and Germany, and the other to Linz, Austria. The third mission escorted B-24 Liberator bombers of the 55BW to, over, and from the marshalling yards at Muhldorf. At least one of the pilots reported seeing an enemy jet-propelled aircraft over the Brenner Pass between Italy and Austria.

March 20: The 332FG flew three missions. One escorted a Mosquito type aircraft on a photographic reconnaissance mission over Linz, Austria and Munich, Germany, one to escort a C-47 transport type aircraft over Sanki Most, Yugoslavia, and one to escort B-24 bombers in the second wave of 304BW bombers to Kralupy oil refinery in Czechoslovakia. On the bomber escort mission, Flight Officer Newman C. Golden of the 99FS was reported missing after bailing out of his mechanically damaged P-51B aircraft at 1132 hours over Wels, Austria.

March 21: The 332FG flew four missions. One escorted B-24 bombers of the 47BW to an airdrome at Neuberg, Germany. The other three missions escorted P-38 aircraft on photographic reconnaissance missions over Linz, Austria; Munich, Germany; Nurnberg, Germany; and Prague, Czechoslovakia.

March 22: P-51 fighters of the 332FG flew two missions, one to escort one P-38 airplane on a photographic reconnaissance mission over Ruhland, Germany. On that mission, one of the P-51s was damaged by enemy antiaircraft artillery fire. The other 332FG mission escorted two waves of B-24 bombers of the 304BW to, over, and from the Kralupy oil refinery in Czechoslovakia.

March 23: The 332FG escorted two waves of B-17s of the 5BW to, over, and from the Ruhland oil refinery, Germany. 2nd Lt Lincoln T. Hudson of the 301FS was reported missing with his P-51C at 1310 hours northeast of Vienna, Austria, after suffering engine trouble.

March 23-24: The 366th Air Service Squadron at Ramitelli was able to overcome a shortage of 110-gallon fuel tanks in order to supply them to the 332FG for a long mission to Berlin on March 24. Documents suggest that the 366th Air Service Squadron obtained the wing tanks from the 55th Air Service Squadron.

March 24: The 332FG took part in the longest World War II raid of the Fifteenth Air Force. Along with other fighter groups of the Fifteenth Air Force, it escorted B-17 bombers of the 5BW on a mission to Berlin. On the way the Tuskegee Airmen encountered German jet Me-262 fighters and shot down three of them. The three victors were 1st Lt Roscoe Brown, 1st Lt Earl R. Lane, and 2nd Lt Charles V. Brantley, all of whom belonged to the 100FS. For this mission, the 332FG earned its only Distinguished Unit Citation of World War II. The group's 99FS earned its third Distinguished Unit Citation for this mission. Five members of the 31FG's 308FS also each shot down a German jet. Missing Air Crew Reports indicate five 332FG P-51 fighters as missing. The pilots included Capt Armour G. McDaniel and 2nd Lts Ronald Reeves and Robert C. Robinson of the 100FS and Flight Officers

James T. Mitchell Jr. and Leon W. Spears of the 301FS. McDaniel, commander of the 301FS, was shot down by enemy aircraft, and Spears might have been, as well, south of Berlin, at about 1215 hours. Reeves and Robinson ran out of fuel over the Udine area of northern Italy at about 1400 hours, and Mitchell probably experienced mechanical failure south of Chemnitz, Germany, at 1315 hours. Enemy fighters also shot down three of the escorted bombers. A combination of enemy antiaircraft artillery and enemy aircraft shot down two additional escorted bombers. The *Chicago Defender* newspaper published an article stating that the 332FG had flown its 200th mission without losing any bombers, despite the fact that group-escorted bombers had been shot down by enemy airplanes the previous summer. A bomber under the escort of the 332FG had not been shot down by enemy aircraft since late August 1944, a period of seven months. For their heroic actions on this day, 1st Lt Earl R. Lane and 2nd Lt Charles V. Brantley, both of the 100FS, each earned a Distinguished Flying Cross (Roscoe Brown, the other pilot with an aerial victory credit over a jet this day, had already earned a Distinguished Flying Cross for an earlier mission).

March 25: Despite the very long mission of the previous day, the 332FG flew two missions, one to escort a P-38 on a photographic reconnaissance mission over Linz, Austria, and one to escort B-24 Liberator bombers of the 49BW to, over, and from the Prague/Nbely Airdrome in Czechoslovakia. One witness saw what appeared to be a Russian aircraft attacking the P-51s.

March 26: The 332FG again flew two missions, one to escort a Mosquito type aircraft on a photographic reconnaissance mission over Munich, Germany, and one to escort B-17 Flying Fortress bombers to, over, and from the Wiener Neustadt marshalling yards.

March 29: 2nd Lt Roland M. Moody of the 301FS died while serving overseas.

March 30: The 332FG sent P-51s to escort a P-38 on a photographic reconnaissance mission over Munich, Germany.

March 31: The 332FG conducted a fighter sweep and strafing mission against railroad and other targets in the Munich area of southern Germany. During the mission, 12 members of the group shot down a total of 13 enemy airplanes, including FW-190s and Me-109s. The victors included 1st Lt Robert W. Williams, who shot down two FW-190s, and Maj William A. Campbell, 1st Lts Roscoe C. Brown, Earl R. Lane, and Daniel L. Rich, 2nd Lts Raul W. Bell, Thomas P. Brasswell, John W. Davis, James L. Hall, Hugh J. White, and Bertram W. Wilson Jr., and Flight Officer John H. Lyle, who each shot down one enemy aircraft. Three 332FG P-51D pilots were reported missing, including 2nd Lt Arnett W. Starks Jr. and 1st Lt Clarence N. Driver of the 100FS, and 2nd Lt Frank N. Wright of the 99FS. Driver went missing at 1315 hours over northern Italy probably because of low fuel. Wright went into a spin while in pursuit of the enemy at 1420 hours over Landshut, Germany. Starks was hit by enemy antiaircraft artillery at 1430 hours over Voklammerkt, Germany. 1st Lt Robert W. Williams and Bertram W. Wilson Jr., both of the 100FS, each earned a Distinguished Flying Cross for heroic actions on this day.

March: During that month, members of the 332FG and its squadrons shot down a total of 17 enemy airplanes.

April 1: Seven members of the 332FG's 301FS shot down a total of 12 enemy airplanes during a mission to escort B-24s of the 47BW to raid the St.

Polten marshalling yard and conduct a fighter sweep of Linz, Austria. The victors included 1st Lt Harry T. Stewart, who shot down three FW-190s, 1st Lt Charles L. White, who shot down two Me-109s, 2nd Lt Carl E. Carey, who shot down two FW-190s, 2nd Lt John E. Edwards, who shot down two Me-109s, 2nd Lt Walter P. Manning and Harold M. Morris, who each shot down one FW-190, and Flight Officer James H. Fisher, who shot down another FW-190. Two of the 332FG P-51 pilots were reported missing: 2nd Lt Walter P. Manning and Flight Officer William P. Armstrong, both of the 301FS, at 1400 over Wels, Austria, after encountering enemy aircraft. The 332FG sent a set of P-51s on a second mission, to escort a single P-38 on a photographic reconnaissance mission over Prague, Czechoslovakia. For their heroic actions on this date, 1st Lts Charles L. White, John E. Edwards, Harry T. Stewart Jr., and 2nd Lt Carl E. Carey, all of the 301FS, each earned a Distinguished Flying Cross.

April 2: The 332FG flew three missions. Two escorted P-38s on photographic reconnaissance missions, one to the San Severo area of Italy and one to the Munich area of southern Germany. On the Munich mission, they encountered an Me-262 German jet fighter, which attacked the small formation. On the third mission the 332FG escorted B-24 Liberator bombers of the 304BW over the Krems marshalling yards in Austria .

April 5: 332FG P-51 fighters escorted a P-38 on a photographic reconnaissance mission over Linz, Austria, while other group fighters, on another mission, escorted B-17s Flying Fortress bombers of the 5BW on a raid against a major enemy airfield at Udine, Italy.

April 5: The 115th AAF Base Unit, which supported the 477BG, moved from Godman Field, Kentucky, to Freeman Field, Indiana, where the

387th Air Service Group was already located.

April 5-7: African American officers of the 477BG at Freeman Field, Indiana, repeatedly attempted to enter an officers' club that was closed to them, and 61 of them were arrested. Col Robert Selway, commander of the group, released all but three of the officers, who had used force to enter the club. He later prepared a statement for all base personnel to sign regarding separate admission policy for the two officers' clubs on the field.

April 6: The 332FG flew two missions, one to escort B-24 Liberators of the 304th and 47BWs to, over, and from the Verona ordnance depot and marshalling yards in northern Italy, and the other to escort a P-38 on a photographic reconnaissance mission over Prague, Czechoslovakia. The 96th Air Service Group, which had provided ground services for the 332FG in Italy, was inactivated, along with the 366th Air Service Squadron, which also served at Ramitelli. The 523rd Air Service Group was activated at Ramitelli, with many of the same personnel who had been in the 96th Air Service Group or the 366th Air Service Squadron.

April 6: Freeman Field was made a Control Base, and base functions changed. The 387th Air Service Group was made responsible only for the supply and maintenance of the 477BG, and its squadrons were moved to another part of the base, which lowered group morale.

April 7: The 332FG again flew two missions. One escorted six groups of 5BW B-17s raiding the Vipiteno, Camp Di Trens, and Bressanone railroad bridges in northern Italy. One of the group P-51 fighter pilots was initially reported missing, but he later returned. On the second mission, 332FG P-51s escorted a P-38 on a photographic reconnaissance mission over Munich, Germany. 2 Lt Ferrier H. White of the 100FS died while serving overseas. Meanwhile, back in the states, Col Robert Selway of the 477BG ordered the arrest of approximately 100 black officers who refused to sign a paper acknowledging his separate officers' clubs policy at Freeman Field, Indiana.

April 8: The 332FG flew three missions. One escorted a Mosquito-type aircraft on a photographic reconnaissance mission over the Linz and Munich areas of Austria and southern Germany. Another escorted a P-38 on a similar photographic reconnaissance mission over Prague, Yugoslavia. The third mission escorted B-17 Flying Fortresses of three groups of the 5BW on a raid against the Campdazzo railroad bridge in northern Italy. On that mission, one of the B-17s was seen to crash into the Adriatic Sea. The mission report noted that "Bombers were strung out making them difficult to cover."

April 9: The 332FG again flew three missions in one day. The first escorted a P-38 airplane on a photographic reconnaissance mission over the Linz and Nurnberg areas of Austria and Germany. On that mission an enemy Me-262 was seen. On the second mission, group P-51 fighters escorted another P-38 on a photographic reconnaissance mission over the Linz and Prague areas of Austria and Czechoslovakia. On the third 332FG mission of the day, Tuskegee-trained pilots escorted B-17s of the 5BW and B-24s of the 304BW to and from the vicinity of Bologna in northern Italy. On that mission, a B-17 was seen spinning down, with three crewmen parachuting out of it.

April 10: The 332FG flew two missions. One of them escorted B-17s of the 5BW and B-24s of the 304BW on a raid to Bologna, Italy. The other escorted a P-38 on a photographic reconnaissance mission over the Munich area of southern Germany.

April 10: The 115th AAF Base Unit was discontinued, but the 387th Air Service Group remained to take up its functions, supporting the 477BG.

April 10-11: Approximately 100 African American officers of the 477BG refused a second time to sign a new April 9, 1945 regulation issued by Col Robert Selway, commander of the group, stating his policy for separate admission for the two officers' clubs at Freeman Field. The black officers were arrested and later, on April 13, sent to Godman Field under arrest.

April 11: The 332FG flew two missions again. One escorted B-24 Liberators of the 304BG to the Ponte Gardena railroad bridge in northern Italy. The mission report noted that the bombers were strung out, making them difficult to cover. The second mission of the day escorted a P-38 on a photographic reconnaissance mission over Munich, Germany.

April 12: The 332FG flew four missions in one day. Two of them escorted photographic reconnaissance aircraft, one over Linz, Austria and one over Munich, Germany. The other two missions escorted B-24 Liberator bombers, one for the 47BW on a raid against the Casarsa Diversion railroad bridge of northern Italy, and one for the 49BW against the St. Veit railroad bridge. On the last mission, two of the escorting P-51s collided. One pilot was reported lost, and the other one was reported as missing. 2nd Lt Samuel G. Leftenant of the 99FS was reported missing with his P-51C at 1508 hours north of Klagenfurth after the mid-air collision.

April 14: The 332FG flew two missions. One escorted a photographic reconnaissance aircraft over Munich in southern Germany. The other escorted four British Halifax bombers of the 148th Squadron (Royal Air Force) to, over, and from Voschia. The British bombers dropped supplies

1st Lt. Francis B. Collier, Wing Interim Training Officer.

to friendly personnel on the ground.

April 15: The 332FG flew three missions. The first escorted a single P-38 on a photographic reconnaissance mission over Bolzano and Prague, Czechoslovakia. The second escorted B-24 bombers of the 304BW ("Blue Force" section) to, over, and from an ammunition factory and storage facility at Ghedi. The third mission strafed railroad targets in the areas of Munich, Salzburg, Linz, Pilzen, and Regensburg in Germany and Austria. On this last mission, Lt Jimmy Lanham of the 301FS shot down an Me-109 in the Munich area. One of the 332FG pilots was reported lost, one was reported missing, and two were reported to have landed at friendly fields. There are missing air crew reports on Flight Officers Morris E. Gant and Thurston L. Gaines, both of the 99FS, who flew P-51Cs. Gaines went missing at 1430 hours about 40 miles from Muhl-

dorf, Germany after being hit by enemy antiaircraft artillery fire, and Gant was reported missing at 1600 hours about 12 miles east of Pescara, Italy, after running low on fuel. For his leadership of this outstanding railroad strafing mission, in which the 332FG destroyed or damaged 35 locomotives, eight oil cars, 44 other units of rolling stock, four barges, four motor transports on a flat car, and one aircraft in the air, Col Benjamin O. Davis earned the only Silver Star awarded to any member of the 332FG. For their heroic actions on this day, Capt Gordon M. Rapier and 1st Lt Jimmy Lanham of the 301FS and Capt William A. Campbell and 1st Lt Gentry E. Barnes of the 99FS each earned the Distinguished Flying Cross.

April 16: The 332FG flew five missions in one day. The first escorted three C-47 transports that went to northern Yugoslavia. Three of the missions escorted P-38s on photographic reconnaissance missions to the Munich and Linz areas of southern Germany and Austria. The other mission escorted B-24 Liberators of the 49th and 55BWs to the Bologna area of northern Italy. The latter mission report noted that the bombers were "strung out and difficult to cover."

April 17: The 332FG flew two missions, one to escort a P-38 on a photographic reconnaissance mission over the Linz area of Austria and the Munich area of southern Germany. The other escorted B-17s of the 5BW and B-24s of the 304BW over and from Bologna, Italy. The report noted that the B-24s were split up by enemy antiaircraft artillery fire in the target area, and fighter coverage was quite difficult.

April 18: The 332FG again flew two missions. One escorted a P-38 on a photographic reconnaissance mission over the Brno area. The other escorted B-24s of the 304BW (although originally assigned to escort B-17s of the 5BW) over and from Bologna, Italy.

April 19: The 332FG flew two missions, one to escort B-24 Liberator bombers to, over, and from the Pucheim railroad yards and Wels, and one to escort a P-38 on a photographic reconnaissance mission over the Munich area of southern Germany.

April 20: The 332FG again flew two missions, one to escort B-24s of the 49 and 55BWs raiding railroad bridges in northern Italy, and one to escort a P-38 on a photographic reconnaissance mission over the Praha and Brno areas of Czechoslovakia. On the first mission, one of the P-51 pilots was at first reported missing, but he eventually returned.

April 21: The 332FG flew three missions in one day. It flew a fighter sweep south of a line running from Augsburg to Munich to Regensburg. Another mission escorted B-24 Liberators of the 49BW to, over, and from the Attang and Pucheim marshalling yards. The third mission escorted two British bombers, one Halifax and one Lancaster, on a supply-dropping mission over Yugoslavia. Flight Officer Leland H. Pennington of the 301FS was reported missing with his P-51B at 1050 hours 15 miles west of Zara off the coast of Yugoslavia. 1st Lt Hugh J. White of the 99FS was also reported missing on April 21. He returned eight days later, having evaded enemy forces in Italy.

April 22: The 332FG was assigned to escort a pho-

tographic reconnaissance aircraft over Brno, Czechoslovakia. The group conducted an armed reconnaissance mission over northern Italy. This was the 300th mission the 332FG flew for the Fifteenth Air Force.

April 23: The 332FG flew three missions, one to escort a P-38 on a reconnaissance mission over the Prague area of Czechoslovakia, one to escort another P-38 on another reconnaissance mission over the Linz and Brno areas, and one to escort B-24 Liberators of the 55 and 304BWs to and over the Padua and Cavarzere areas of Italy. On the latter mission one of the 332FG P-51 fighters was hit by enemy antiaircraft artillery, but the pilot bailed out safely. He was 1st Lt Hugh J. White of the 99FS, who was reported missing at 1150 hours over Stanghella, Italy.

April 24: The 332FG escorted B-24 bombers of the 47 and 49BWs to, over, and from enemy targets in northern Italy.

April 25: The 332FG flew four missions, including one armed reconnaissance mission over the Verona area of northern Italy. Two other missions escorted Mosquito-type aircraft on reconnaissance missions, one over the Munich area of southern Germany and one over the Linz area of Austria. The fourth mission escorted a P-38 on a reconnaissance mission over the Salzburg area of Austria.

April 26: The 332FG flew two missions. One escorted a P-38 on a reconnaissance mission over Linz, Prague, and Amstettin in central Europe. On that mission, the group encountered German Me-109 fighters. 2nd Lt Thomas W. Jefferson shot down two of the enemy airplanes, and 1st Lt Jimmy Lanham and 2nd Lt Richard A. Simons each shot down one. These were the last aerial victories of the Tuskegee Airmen during the war. The 332FG had shot down a total of

94 enemy aircraft during World War II. The 99FS had shot down a total of 18 enemy airplanes before joining the 332FG. Together, African American pilots shot down a total of 112 enemy airplanes during World War II. The other mission was the 332FG's final bomber escort for the Fifteenth Air Force, protecting B-24s of the 47 and 55BWs on raids over the Casarsa and Malcontenta ammunition storage dumps. 1st Lt Thomas W. Jefferson of the 301FS earned a Distinguished Flying Cross for his heroic actions on this day.

Top Brass assembled at Cattolica, Italy, in May 1945. From left: Maj Gen Nathan Twining, Col Benjamin O. Davis Jr., Brig Gen Dean C. Strother, and Brig Gen Yantis H. Taylor, respectively commanders of the 15th Air Force; 332nd Fighter Group; 15th Fighter Command; and 306th Fighter Wing.

April 26-27: In the United States, the 477BG and its four squadrons (616th, 617th, 618th, and 619th) moved from Freeman Field, Indiana, where there had been a racial incident, back to Godman Field, Kentucky, where the group had been based before March 5.

April 28: The 387th Air Service Group moved back from Freeman Field, Indiana, to Godman Field, Kentucky, where it had been stationed before March 7.

April 30: The 332FG flew its 311th mission for the Fifteenth Air Force, providing escort for a reconnaissance aircraft to Bolzano, Italy. Since the 332FG was assigned to the Fifteenth Air Force, which managed U.S. strategic bombing in the Mediterranean Theater of Operations, the group had flown 179 bomber escort mis-

sions, 172 of them to protect heavy bombers such as B-17s or B-24s. This is the last 332FG mission for the Fifteenth Air Force for which a mission report was found.

April : During this month members of the 332FG and its squadrons shot down a total of 17 enemy airplanes.

May 1: The 332FG was scheduled to launch 48 P-51s to escort bombers to Klagenfurt, Austria, and also to escort a reconnaissance mission over San Severo, Italy, but no narrative mission reports for these missions have been found. The 332FG might have flown more than 311 missions for the Fifteenth Air Force, but no reports on other missions were found.

May 4: The 332FG moved from Ramitelli Airfield, Italy, to Cattolica, Italy.

May 6: 1st Lt Hugh J. White of the 99FS returned to his unit after repatriation from northern Italy. An armada of "Red Tails" took part in a Fifteenth Air Force Review over Caserta and Bari, Italy. A note in the Fifteenth Air Force mission folder for May 6, 1945 notes that "48 P-51s of the 332FG taking off at 0800 will intercept 304th Wing at 0912 and provide close escort on PTW." (penetration, target cover, and withdrawal). No mission report was found to confirm that the plan was executed.

May 7: P-51 pilots of the 332FG flew through the Brenner Pass between Italy and Austria and then over the Linz airdrome in Austria to test whether the Germans would honor the armistice they signed.

May 8: The 332FG held a ceremony to celebrate VE (Victory in Europe) Day. During this ceremony, Col Yantis H. Taylor, commander of the 306th Fighter Wing, awarded honors to 332FG personnel.

May 10: Flight Officers James T. Mitchell and Leon W. Spears of the 301FS returned to their unit after repatriation from Poland.

May 11: 2nd Lt James L. Hall Jr. of the 99FS returned to his unit after repatriation from Romania. The 332FG assembled for a ceremony in which Maj Gen Nathan F. Twining, commander of the Fifteenth Air Force, presented various honors, including the Distinguished Flying Cross, the Air Medal, and the Bronze Star, to various members of the 332FG.

May 29: Maj William A. Campbell was awarded the first oak leaf cluster to his Distinguished Flying Cross, becoming the first black pilot to earn two DFCs.

May 30: The 332FG held a Memorial Day ceremony to honor members of the organization who died during the war. The program included a reading of the Gettysburg Address.

June 1: The 67th AAF Base Unit (Tuskegee Weather Detachment) was discontinued.

June 8: In an impressive ceremony, Col Yantis H. Taylor, commander of the 306th Fighter Wing, presented Col Benjamin O. Davis Jr., commander of the 332FG, the Silver Star for gallantry in action. He also awarded five Distinguished Flying Crosses, five Air Medals, and one Bronze Star. The troops passed in review to bid farewell to Col Davis as commander, who departed for the United States. Col Davis had been chosen to command the 477th Composite Group at God-

man Field, Kentucky. In his farewell speech, Col Davis noted that the 332FG had been a credit to itself and the Army Air Forces.

June 9: Maj George S. Roberts resumed command of the 332FG.

June 12: The 332FG was relieved of its assignment to the XV Fighter Command (Provisional).

June 21: Col Benjamin O. Davis Jr. assumed command of the 477 BG, replacing Col Robert R. Selway Jr. Davis also became temporary commander of the 387th Air Service Group, which supported the 477BG at Godman Field. Davis replaced Lt Col David H. Thomas, a white officer who had been in command of the 387th Air Service Group since July 1944.

June 22: The 99FS moved to Godman Field, Kentucky, and was reassigned from the 332FG to the 477th Group, which was redesignated from a Bombardment Group to a Composite Group, since it would have both bombers and fighters. The 616 and the 619BSs of the group were inactivated, but the 617 and 618BSs remained.

June 26: Maj Elmer D. Jones Jr. assumed command of the 387th Air Service Group, relieving Lt Col Benjamin O. Davis Jr., who remained commander of the 477BG.

June 29: The emblem of the 301FS was approved. It consisted of a disk depicting a cat on a flying machine gun.

c. July 18: The 332FG moved from Cattolica, Italy, to Lucera, Italy.

September: The 332FG departed Lucera, Italy, for movement to the United States.

October 4: The War Department directed that a three-man board of officers prepare a policy for the use of Negro manpower in the post-war period, "including the complete development of the means required to derive the maximum efficiency from the full authorized manpower of the nation…"

October 8: The 618BS was inactivated, leaving the 477 Composite Group with only two squadrons, the 99FS and the 617BS.

October 17: The 332FG arrived at Camp Kilmer, New Jersey.

October 19: The 332FG was inactivated, along with the 100FS and the 301FS. The 302FS had already been inactivated in March. That left only the 99FS active, and it had already been assigned to the 477th Composite Group.

November 17: A War Department board of general officers headed by Lt Gen Alvan C. Gillem Jr. submitted a report, "Policy for Utilization of Negro Manpower in the Post-War Army" to U.S. Army Chief of Staff, Gen George C. Marshall. Besides Gen Gillem, Maj Gen Lewis A. Pick and Brig. Gen. Winslow C. Morse served on the board. Although the report called for more Negro officers, more Negro combat units, more opportunities for professional and leadership development for Negroes, equal treatment of all officers, and continued "experimental groupings of Negro units with white units in composite organizations," it did not call for immediate or complete desegregation of the Army.

November 28: In a memorandum to Secretary of War Robert B. Patterson, Truman K. Gibson Jr., civilian aide to the Secretary of War, criticized the Gillem Report for failing to clearly address the issue of segregation and called for the War Department to issue a clear policy

statement on the issue.

1946

March 13: The 99FS moved to Lockbourne Army Air Base, Ohio, along with the 477th Composite Group to which it was assigned.

April 14: The 2143rd AAF Base Unit (Pilot School, Basic-Advanced) was discontinued at TAAF, but the field did not close yet, and the last class, (46-C) continued training there.

April 15: The 385th AAF Base Unit was organized at TAAF, Alabama, replacing the 2143nd AAF Base Unit that had served there.

June 29: The last class of pilots (46-C) graduated at TAAF.

June 30: TAAF was placed on temporarily inactive status, with permanent inactivation to come, because personnel were still assigned to the base.

August 20: Col Noel F. Parrish was reassigned from TAAF, which he had commanded, to Air University at Maxwell Field, Alabama.

Civil Air Patrol landed at Lockbourne AFB.

Personnel of the 332nd Fighter Wing planted a tree at Lockbourne AFB on February 22, 1949, to commemorate George Washington's birthday.

August 31: Lt Col Donald G. McPherson assumed command of the 385th AAF Base Unit, the only unit remaining at TAAF.

September 1: The training department at TAAF inactivated. It had remained active after pilot training at Tuskegee ended (June 29) in order to provide continuation flying training of rated personnel still stationed there.

1947

June 12: TAAF closed permanently when the 385th AAF Base Unit, the last unit there, was discontinued.

July 1: The 477th Composite Group and the 617 BS, which had been assigned to it, were inactivated at AAB Lockbourne, Ohio. The 99FS, which had also been assigned to the 477th Composite Group, was reassigned to the newly reactivated 332FG at Lockbourne. The inactivated 100 and 301FSs were activated again, and assigned, like the 99FS, to the 332FG. The group and its squadrons were equipped with P-47 aircraft.

July 28: The 332FW was established, but not yet activated.

August 15: The 332FW was activated under the command of Maj Edward C. Gleed at Lockbourne Army Air Base. The 332FG was assigned to the wing. The honors of the group were bestowed on the like-numbered wing under which it served, but the group retained all of those honors as well.

October-November: The 99FS of the 332FG (332FW) took part in Operation Combine and performed so well that it was awarded a certificate of appreciation signed by Maj Gen William

D. Old, commander of the Ninth Air Force. The certificate noted that the squadron's personnel worked under difficulties and handicaps not normally expected, but in spite of them, performed with exceptionally high efficiency. Operation Combine was a training exercise involving a simulated invasion of the United States, and involved the dropping of airborne forces and tactical air support for them.

1948

July 26: President Harry S. Truman signed Executive Order 9981, which stated "It is hereby declared to be the policy of the President that there shall be equality of treatment and opportunity for all persons in the Armed Services without regard to race..." The same order called for the creation within the National Military Establishment of "an advisory committee to be known as the President's Committee on Equality of Treatment and Opportunity in the Armed Services..." which he authorized to examine the "rules, procedures, and practices of the Armed Services... to determine in what respect such rules, procedures, and practices may be altered or improved with a view to carrying out the policy of this order." While the order did not specifically mention the words "integration" or "desegregation," that is what resulted. The U. S. Air Force had already announced in April that it would integrate, and that was accomplished in May 1949.

October 8: The 387th Air Service Group was inactivated and disbanded at Godman Field, Kentucky.

1949

January 20: Members of the 332FG took part, as ordered by 332 FW Special Order 15 dated January 19, 1949, in the inaugural parade for President Harry S. Truman, who had in the previous year issued Executive Order 9981 calling for equality of treatment and opportunity in the armed services.

May 2-11: At the 1949 USAF Gunnery Meet in Las Vegas, Nevada, the 332FG team won top honors in the conventional aircraft division. Among the victors were Capt Alva N. Temple, Lt James H. Harvey Jr., and Lt Harry T. Stewart Jr.

May 11: The Department of the Air Force issued Air Force Letter No. 35-3, which noted that "all Negroes will not necessarily be assigned to Negro units. Qualified Negro personnel may be assigned to fill any position vacancy in any Air Force organization or overhead installation without regard to race." The same letter noted "All individuals, regardless of race, will be accorded equal opportunity for appointment, advancement, professional improvement, promotion, and retention in all components of the Air Force of the United States." The U.S. Air Force was the first of the armed services to officially integrate.

July 1: The 332FG and its three fighter squadrons, the 99th, 100th, and 301st, were inactivated. Members of those organizations were reassigned to other organizations that became racially integrated.

PRIMARY SOURCES

Periodic histories of the 99FS located at the Air Force Historical Research Agency with the call number SQ-FI-99-HI followed by the month.

Monthly histories of the 332FG, which include the daily mission reports of the group, located at the Air Force Historical Research Agency with the call number GP-332-HI followed by the month.

Tuskegee Airmen win "Top Gun" competition., May 1949.

Monthly histories of the 477BG, located at the Air Force Historical Research Agency with the call number GP-477-HI followed by the month.

Fifteenth Air Force daily mission reports located at the Air Force Historical Research Agency with the call number 670.332 followed by the date.

Missing Air Crew Reports at the Air Force Historical Research Agency, on microfiche, filed by number and indexed on paper, the index showing by date which numbered air force and group lost aircraft, with the type of the aircraft, the serial number, and the location. Each missing air crew report notes the group and squadron to which the aircraft belonged, the date and time the aircraft was lost, the place the aircraft was lost, and the cause of the loss.

Organizational Record cards and lineage and honors histories of the organizations to which the Tuskegee Airmen belonged, including the 332FG, and its four fighter squadrons, the 99th, 100th, 301st, and 302nd, and the 477th Bombardment Group and its four bombardment squadrons, the 616th, 617th, 618th, and 619th.

Twelfth Air Force General Orders (for aerial victory credits and Distinguished Flying Cross awards) located at Air Force Historical Research Agency with call number 650.193.

Fifteenth Air Force General Orders (for aerial victory credits and Distinguished Flying Cross awards) located at Air Force Historical Research Agency with call number 670.193.

SECONDARY SOURCES

Davis, Benjamin O. Jr., *Benjamin O. Davis, Jr.: American* (Washington, DC: Smithsonian Institution Press, 1991).

Hardesty, Von *Black Wings* (Washington, DC: Smithsonian Institution Press, 2008).

Homan, Lynn M., and Thomas Reilly, *Black Knights* (Gretna, LA: Pelican Publishing Company, 2006).

Jakeman, Robert J., *The Divided Skies* (Tuscaloosa: The University of Alabama Press, 1992).

Lee, Ulysses, *The Employment of Negro Troops* (Washington, DC: Office of the Chief of Military History, United States Army, 1966).

Maurer, Maurer, *Combat Squadrons of the Air Force, World War II* (Washington, DC: U.S. Government Printing Office, 1969).

Maurer, Maurer, *Air Force Combat Units of World War II* (Washington, DC: U.S. Government Printing Office, 1983).

Moye, J. Todd, *Freedom Flyers* (Oxford, UK: Oxford University Press, 2010).

President Ronald Reagan, far left, stands with Tuskegee University President Benjamin Payton at the dedication on the Tuskegee campus of the aerospace education center named in honor of Tuskegee Airman Daniel "Chappie" James.

Right: The first Tuskegee Airmen graduates on the flight line with one of their instructors (see class photo on facing page): From left, George S. Roberts; Benjamin O. Davis Jr.; Charles DeBow Jr.; Lieutenant R. M. Long, instructor pilot; Mac Ross; and Lemuel R. Custis.

CLASS PHOTOGRAPHS

This section contains samples of the existing photographs of the graduating classes of pilots in the Tuskegee Airmen program from 1941–1946. Some 992 pilots are known to have completed pilot training at Tuskegee and gone directly to combat operations in North Africa and Italy or else to additional training in single- and multi-engine airplanes at other bases in the U.S.

The first class of black pilots in the history of the United States Army Air Forces graduated at Tuskegee March 7, 1942, when "wings" and commissions were presented by Major General George E. Stratemeyer. From left, Captain B. O. Davis Jr., and 2nd Lieutenants Lemuel R. Custis, George S. Roberts, Charles Debow, and Mac Ross. All were assigned to the 99th Pursuit Squadron. (Davis had a different rank because he was a graduate of West Point and already an Army officer before becoming a Tuskegee Airman.) (See also the photo of these men on the facing page.)

Above: (Class 42-D) (order unknown) Sidney P. Brooks, Charles W. Dryden, Clarence C. Jamison.

Right: (Class 42-E) (order unknown) James B. Knighton, George L. Knox, Lee Rayford, Sherman W. White.

Above: (Class 42-F) William A. Campbell, Willie Ashley, Langston Caldwell, Herbert V. Clark, George R. Bolling, Charles B. Hall, Paul Graham Mitchell, Herbert E. Carter, Louis R. Purnell, Graham P. Smith, Allen G. Lane, Spann Watson, Faythe A. McGinnis, James T. Wiley, Irwin Lawrence.

Right: (Class 42-G) (order unknown) Richard Davis, Willie Fuller, Cassius Harris, Earl E. King, Walter E. Lawson, John H. McClure, Leon C. Roberts, John W. Roberts.

Above: (Class 42-H) Front, Samuel M. Bruce, Wilmore B. Leonard, James L. McCullin, Henry Perry. Back, John H. Morgan, Richard C. Caesar, Edward L. Toppins, Robert W. Deiz, Joseph D. Elsberry.

Below: (Class 42-J) Jerome T. Edwards, Terry J. Charlton, Howard L. Baugh, Melvin T. Jackson.

Top: (Class 42-I) Nathaniel M. Hill, Marshall S. Cabiness, Herman A. Lawson, William T. Mattison, John A. Gibson, Elwood T. Driver, Price D. Rice, Andrew D. Turner.

Bottom: (Class 42-K) (order unknown) Edward C. Gleed, Milton T. Hall, Wendell O. Pruitt, Richard C. Pullam, Peter C. Verwayne, William H. Walker, Romeo M. Williams, Robert B. Tresville Jr.

Right: (Class 43-A) George T. McCrumby, Quitman C. Walker, Andrew Maples, Charles R. Stanton, Clinton B. Mills, Armour G. McDaniel.

Below: (Class 43-B) Roy M. Spencer, Claude B. Govan, James R. Pokinghorne, John R. Prowell, William H. Walker, William E. Griffin, Walter Downs.

Top: (Class 43-C) (order unknown) Clarence W. Allen, Leroy Bowman, Woodrow W. Crockett, Alfonza W. Davis, Lawrence E. Dickson, Alwayne M. Dunlap, Elmer A. Gordon, William M. Gordon, Charles F. Jamerson, Walter L. McCreary, Pearlee E. Sanders, Wilmer W. Sidat-Singh, Lloyd G. Singletary.

Bottom: (Class 43-D) Front, Heber C. Houston, James E. Brothers, Arnold W. Cisco, Paul Adams, William J. Faulkner, Freddie E. Hutchins, Wilson V. Eagleson, Sidney J. Moseley. Back, Ulysses S. Taylor, Harold E. Sawyer, Luke J. Weathers, Lewis C. Smith, Leonard M. Jackson, Curtis C. Robinson, Vernon V. Haywood, James Y. Carter, Walter T. Foreman, Charles P. Bailey, Charles I. Williams.

Top: (Class 43-E) Front, Laurence D. Wilkins, Maurice V. Esters, Oliver O. Miller, Luther H. Smith, Langdon E. Johnson, James A. Walker, John J. Suggs, Clemenceau M. Givings. Back, Joseph P. Gomer, Felix J. Kirkpatrick, Craig H. Williams, George E. Gray, Dempsey W. Morgan, Spurgeon N. Ellington, Albert H. Manning, Dudley M. Watson, Milton R. Brooks, Harry A. Sheppard, Charles M. Bussey, John F. Briggs.

Bottom: (Class 43-F) Front, Willie S. Hunter, Wayne V. Liggins, Hezekiah Lacy, Theodore A. Wilson, Charles E. McGee, Oscar A. Kenney, Richard H. Harris, Weldon K. Groves. Second row, Frank D. Walker, Joe A. Lewis, Wilbert H. Johnson, William F. Williams, Leonard F. Turner, William G. Wilkerson. Back, John S. Sloan, Walter J. Palmer, Theopolis D. Moore, Wiley W. Selden, Robert R. Alexander, Herbert S. Harris, Milton R. Henry, Alexander M. Bright.

Top: (Class 43-G) Front, Lowell C. Steward, William R. Melton Jr., Walter D. Westmoreland, Maurice R. Page, Elmer W. Taylor, Jack D. Holsclaw, Eddie A. McLaurin, Cornelius G. Rogers, William W. Green, George B. Greenlee Jr., Clayborne A. Lockett, John Daniels. Back, Lee A. Archer, William B. Ellis, Alva N. Temple, William R. Bartley, LeRoi S. Williams, James W. Mason, Beryl Wyatt, Daniel James Jr., Edward M. Smith, Robert H. Nelson, John H. Leahr, Harry L. Bailey, Richard E. Hall, Robert H. Wiggins, Samuel L. Curtis.

Bottom: (Class 43-H) (order unknown) Alton F. Ballard, Hubron R. Blackwell, Everett A. Bratcher, Harry J. Daniels, Andrew H. Doswell, Charles A. Dunne, Smith W. Green, William E. Hill, Lawrence B. Jefferson, Samuel Jefferson, Hubert L. Jones, William B. McClenic Jr., Starling B. Penn, Leon Purchase, Roger Romine, Norvel Stoudmire, George A. Taylor, Charles W. Tate, Floyd A. Thompson, Carol S. Woods, Willard L. Woods, Alex Pasquet.

Top: (Class 43-I) (order unknown) William N. Alsbrook, Cecil L. Browder, Gene Cole Browne, William Cross Jr., Purnell J. Goodenough, George J. Haley, Maceo A. Harris Jr., Carl E. Johnson, Charles B. Johnson, Edgar L. Jones, Carroll N. Langston Jr., Cornelius F. May, Woodrow F. Morgan, Neal V. Nelson, Christopher W. Newman, Driskell B. Ponder, George M. Rhodes Jr., Washington D. Ross, Norman W. Scales, Henry B. Scott, Alphonso Simmons, Robert H. Smith, Edward Wilson Watkins.

Bottom: (Class 43-J) (order unknown) James B. Brown, Roger B. Brown, Herman R. Campbell Jr., Alfred Q. Carroll Jr., Clarence W. Dart, Charles W. Dickerson, Henri F. Fletcher, Perry E. Hudson Jr., Oscar D. Hutton, Haldane King, Edward Laird, Ivey L. Leftwich, Vincent J. Mason, Theodore H. Mills, Turner W. Payne, Gwynne W. Peirson, Harvey N. Pinkney, Nathaniel P. Rayburg, Emory L. Robbins Jr., Earl S. Sherard Jr., Paul C. Simmons Jr., Eugene D. Smith, Jerome D. Spurlin, Nathaniel C. Stewart, Edward M. Thomas, William H. Thomas, William D. Tompkins, Hugh St. Clair Warner, Leslie A. Williams.

Top: (Class 43-K) (order unknown) Edgar L. Bolden, Clarence H. Bradford, Robert H. Daniels Jr., Othel Dickson, Robert J. Friend, Frederick D. Funderburg, Howard C. Gamble, Stanley L. Harris, Llyod S. Hathcock, Wellington O. Irving, Clarence D. Lester, Willaim R. Lewis, Henry Pollard, Reid E. Thompson, William L. Hill, Edward Julius Williams, Elmore M. Kennedy, Fitzroy Newsum, Samuel A. Black Jr., Harold E. Brazil, Willie L. Byrd Jr., Eugene C. Cheatham, Stewart B. Fulbright Jr., John L. Harrison Jr., Henry P. Hervey Jr., Richard B. Highbaugh, Harold A. Hillary, Samuel Lynn, Joseph D. Whiten, Amos A. Rogers, Wendell D. Wells.

Bottom: (Class 44-A) (order unknown) Clarence N. Driver, Charles H. Duke, Charles S. Jackson Jr., Alexander Jefferson, Robert L. Martin, Frederick D. McIlver Jr., Robert O'Neil, Sanford M. Perkins, Frank E. Roberts, Arthur J. Wilburn, Charles H. Hunter, Frederick L. Parker Jr., Leon L. Turner, Elliott H. Blue, Rolin A. Bynum, Virgil A. Daniels, Samuel W. Harper, Kenneth R. Hawkins, Andrea P. Masciana, William A. Rucker, Saint M. Twine Jr., Charles E. Walker, Clarence Williams, Herbert W. Williams, Eugene Winslow.

EMBLEMS OF TUSKEGEE AIRMEN UNITS

332nd Fighter Group

99th Fighter Squadron

100th Fighter Squadron

301st Fighter Squadron

302nd Fighter Squadron

616th Bombardment Squadron

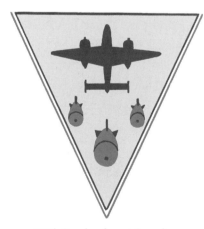

617th Bombardment Squadron

618th Bombardment Squadron

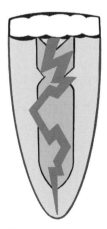

619th Bombardment Squadron

216

TUSKEGEE AIRMEN PILOT ROSTER

This list contains the names of the men known to have completed pilot training and served as Tuskegee Airmen, 1941–1946. (This list is not included in the index.)

(H) = Haitian
(V) = Virgin Islands

Adams, John H.
Adams, Paul
Adkins, Rutherford H.
Adkins, Winston A.
Alexander, Halbert L.
Alexander, Harvey R.
Alexander, Robert R.
Alexander, Walter G. II
Allen, Carl V.
Allen, Clarence W.
Allen, Walter H.
Allison, James M.
Alsbrook, William N.
Alston, William R.
Anders, Emet R.
Anderson, Paul T.
Anderson, Rayfield A.
Anderson, Robert D.
Archer, Lee A., Jr
Armistead, Richard S. A.
Armstrong, William P.
Ashby, Robert
Ashley, Willie
Askins, Montro C.
Audant, Ludovic F.
Bailey, Charles P.
Bailey, Harry L.

Bailey, Terry C.
Bailey, William H.
Baldwin, Henry Jr.
Ballard, Alton F.
Barksdale, James M.
Barland, Herbert C.
Barnes, Gentry E.
Barnett, Herman A.
Bartley, William R.
Bates, George A.
Baugh, Howard L.
Bee, Clarence Jr.
Bell, George E.
Bell, John J.
Bell, Lloyd W.
Bell, Richard H.
Bell, Rual W.
Bennett, Joseph B.
Bibb, William V.
Bickham, Luzine B.
Biffle, Richard L., Jr.
Bilbo, Reuben B
Bing, George L.
Black, Samuel A.
Blackwell, Hubron R.
Blaylock, Joseph H.
Blue, Elliott H.
Bohannon, Horace A.
Bohler, Henry C. L.
Bolden, Edgar L.
Bolden, George C.
Bolling, George R.
Bonam, Leonelle A.
Bonseigneur, Paul J., Jr.
Bowman, James E.
Bowman, Leroy
Bradford, Clarence H.
Brantley, Charles V.
Brashears, Virgil
Braswell, Thomas P.
Bratcher, Everett A.
Brazil, Harold E.
Brewin, Irvin O.
Briggs, Eugene A., Jr.
Briggs, John F.
Bright, Alexander M.
Broadnax, Samuel L.

Broadwater, William E.
Brooks, Milton R.
Brooks, Sidney P.
Brooks, Tilford U.
Brothers, James E.
Brothers, James E.
Browder, Cecil L.
Brower, Fred L., Jr.
Brown, Augustus G.
Brown, George A., Jr.
Brown, Harold H.
Brown, Harold H.
Brown, James B.
Brown, James W., Jr.
Brown, Lawrence A.
Brown, Reuben H., Jr.
Brown, Robert S.
Brown, Roger B.
Brown, Roscoe C. Jr.
Brown, Walter R., Jr.
Browne, Gene C.
Bruce, Reginald A.
Bruce, Samuel M.
Bryant, Grady E.
Bryant, Joseph C., Jr
Bryant, Leroy Jr.
Bryson, James O.
Burch, John A. III
Burns, Charles A.
Burns, Isham A., Jr.
Bussey, Charles M.
Butler, Jewel B.
Bynum, Rolin A.
Byrd, Willie L. Jr.
Cabiness, Marshall S.
Cabule, Ernest M., Jr.
Caesar, Richard C.
Cain, William L.
Calhoun, James A.
Calloway, Julius W.
Campbell, Herman R., Jr.
Campbell, Lindsay L.
Campbell, McWheeler
Campbell, Vincent O.
Campbell, William A.
Carey, Carl E.
Carpenter, Russell W.

Carroll, Alfred Q., Jr.
Carroll, Lawrence W.
Carter, Clarence J.
Carter, Floyd J.
Carter, Herbert E.
Carter, James Y.
Carter, Lloyd A. N.
Carter, William G.
Casey, Clifton C.
(H) Cassagnol, Raymond
Chambers, Charles W.
Chandler, Robert C.
Charlton, Terry J.
Chavis, John H.
Cheatham, Eugene C.
Cheek, Conrad H.
Cheek, Quinten V.
Chichester, James R.
Chin, Jack
Chineworth, Joseph E.
Choisy, George B.
Cisco, Arnold W.
Cisco, George E.
Clark, Herbert V.
Clayton, Melvin A.
Claytor, Ralph V.
Cleaver, Lowell H.
Clifton, Emile G., Jr.
Cobbs, Wilson N.
Coggs, Granville C.
Colbert, William A., Jr.
Cole, Robert A.
Coleman, James
Coleman, William C., Jr.
Coleman, William J.
Collins, Gamaliel M.
Collins, Russell L.
Connell, Victor L.
Cook, Martin L.
Cooper, Charles W.
Cooper, Edward M.
Corbin, Matthew J.
Cousins, Augustus J.
Cousins, William M.
Cowan, Edwin T.
Cox, Hannibal M., Jr.
Craig, Charles E.

Craig, Lewis W.
Criss, LeRoy
Crockett, Woodrow W.
Cross, William Jr.
Crumbsy, Grover
Cummings, Herndon M.
Curry, John C.
Curry, Walter P.
Curtis, John W.
Curtis, Samuel L.
Curtis, William J., Jr.
Custis, Lemuel R.
Dabney, Roscoe J., Jr.
Daniels, Harry J.
Daniels, John
Daniels, Robert H., Jr.
Daniels, Thomas J. III
Daniels, Virgil A.
Darnell, Charles E.
Dart, Clarence W.
Davenport, Harry J., Jr.
Davis, Alfonza W.
Davis, Benjamin O., Jr.
Davis, Claude C.
Davis, Clifford W.
Davis, Donald F.
Davis, John W.
Davis, Richard
Davis, Sylvester S., Jr.
Dean, Vincent C.
DeBow, Charles
Deiz, Robert W.
Derricotte, Eugene A.
Desvignes, Russell F.
Dickerson, Charles W.
Dickerson, Page L.
Dickerson, Tamenund J., Jr.
Dickson, Dewitt
Dickson, Lawrence E.
Dickson, Othel
Diggs, Charles W.
Dillard, James M., Jr.
Dillon, Oliver M.
Dixon, Edward T.
Doram, Edward D.
Dorkins, Charles J.

Doswell, Andrew H.
Doswell, Edgar A., Jr.
Dowling, Cornelius D.
Downs, Walter M.
Driver, Clarence N.
Driver, Elwood T.
Drummond, Charles Jr.
Drummond, Edward Jr.
Dryden, Charles W.
Dudley, Richard G.
Duke, Charles H.
Duncan, Roger B.
Dunlap, Alwayne M.
Dunne, Charles A.
Eagleson, Wilson V.
Echols, Julius P.
Edwards, James E., Jr.
Edwards, Jerome T.
Edwards, John E.
Edwards, William H.
Elfalan, Jose R.
Ellington, Spurgeon N.
Ellis, Carl F.
Ellis, Everett M.
Ellis, William B.
Ellsberry, Joseph D.
Esters, Maurice V.
Ewing, James Jr.
Exum, Herven P.
Farley, William H.
Faulkner, William J.
Fears, Henry T.
Finley, Clarence C., Jr.
Finley, Otis B.
Fischer, James H.
Flake, Thomas M.
Fleming, Rutledge H., Jr.
Fletcher, Henri F.
Ford, Harry E., Jr.
Foreman, Samuel J.
Foreman, Walter T.
Francis, William V.
Franklin, Earl N.
Franklin, George E.
Freeman, Eldridge E.
Friend, Robert J.
Fulbright, Stewart B.
Fuller, William A., Jr.
Fuller, Willie H.
Funderburg, Frederick D.
Gaines, Thurston L., Jr.
Gaiter, Roger B.
Gallwey, James H.
Gamble, Howard C.
Gant, Morris E.
Garrett, Alfred E., Jr.
Garrison Jr., Robert E.
Gash, Joseph E.

Gaskins, Aaron C.
Gay, Thomas L.
Gibson, John A.
Giles, Ivie V.
Gilliam, William L.
Givings, Clemenceau M.
Gladden, Thomas
Glass, Robert M.
Gleed, Edward C.
Glenn, Joshua
Goins, Nathaniel W., Jr.
Golden, Newman C.
Goldsby, Charles S.
Gomer, Joseph P.
Goodall, Ollie O., Jr.
Goodenough, Purnell J.
Goodwin, Luther A.
Gordon, Elmer L.
Gordon, Joseph E.
Gordon, William M., Jr.
Gorham, Alfred M.
Gould, Cornelius P., Jr.
Govan, Claude B.
Gray, Elliott H.
Gray, George E.
Gray, Leo R.
Green, James L.
Green, Paul L.
Green, Smith W.
Green, William W. Jr.
Greenlee, George B., Jr.
Greenwell, Jacob W.
Greer, James W.
Griffin, Frank
Griffin, Jerrold D.
Griffin, William E.
Groves, Weldon K.
(H) Guilbaud, Eberle J.
Guyton, Eugene L.
Haley, George J.
Hall, Charles B.
Hall, James L., Jr.
Hall, Leonard C., Jr.
Hall, Milton T.
Hall, Richard W.
Hamilton, John L.
Hancock, Victor L.
Harden, Argonne F.
Harder, Richard S.
Hardy, Bennett G.
Hardy, Ferdinand A.
Hardy, George E.
Harmon, Arthur C.
Harper, Samuel W.
Harris, Alfonso L.
Harris, Archie H., Jr.
Harris, Bernard
Harris, Cassius A.

Harris, Edward
Harris, Herbert S.
Harris, James E.
Harris, John S.
Harris, Louis K.
Harris, Maceo A., Jr.
Harris, Richard H.
Harris, Stanley L.
Harris, Thomas D., Jr.
Harrison, Alvin E., Jr
Harrison, James E.
Harrison, John L., Jr.
Harrison, Lonnie
Harvey, James H., Jr.
Hathcock, Lloyd S.
Hawkins, Donald A.
Hawkins, Kenneth R.
Hawkins, Thomas L.
Hayes, George K.
Hayes, Lee A.
Hays, Milton S.
Hays, Reginald W.
Haywood, Vernon V.
Heath, Percy L., Jr.
Helem, George W.
Henderson, Eugene R.
Henry, Milton R.
Henry, Warren E.
Henry, William T.
Henson, James W.
Herrington, Aaron
Herron, Walter B.
Hervey, Henry P.
Heywood, Herbert H.
Hicks, Arthur N.
Hicks, Frederick P.
Higginbotham, Mitch-
ell L.
Highbaugh, Earl B.
Highbaugh, Richard B.
Hill, Charles A. Jr.
Hill, Charles D.
Hill, Louis G., Jr.
Hill, Nathaniel M.
Hill, William L.
Hill, William E.
Hillary, Harold A.
Hockaday, Wendell W.
Hodges, Jerry T., Jr.
Holbert, Bertrand J.
Holland, Henry T.
Holloman, William H. III
Holloway, Lorenzo W. Jr
Holman, William D.
Holsclaw, Jack D.
Hopson, Vernon
Houston, Heber C.
Hubbard, Lyman L.

Hudson, Elbert
Hudson, Lincoln T.
Hudson, Perry E.
Hughes, Andrew J.
Hughes, Samuel R.
Hunter, Charles H.
Hunter, Henry A.
Hunter, Marcellus L.
Hunter, Samuel C.
Hunter, Willie S.
Hurd, James A.
Hurd, Sylvester H., Jr.
Hurt, Wesley D.
Hutchins, Freddie E.
Hutton, Oscar D., Jr.
Hymes, William H.
Iles, George J.
Irving, Wellington G.
Jackson, Charles L.
Jackson, Charles S., Jr.
Jackson, Donald E.
Jackson, Frank A., Jr.
Jackson, Julien D., Jr.
Jackson, Leonard M.
Jackson, Melvin T.
Jackson, William T.
Jamerson, Charles F.
James, Daniel Jr.
James, Voris S.
Jamison, Clarence C.
Jamison, Donald S.
Jefferson, Alexander
Jefferson, Lawrence B.
Jefferson, Samuel B.
Jefferson, Thomas W.
Jenkins, Edward M.
Jenkins, Garfield L.
Jenkins, Joseph E.
Jenkins, Silas M.
Jenkins, Stephen S., Jr.
Johnson, Alvin J.
Johnson, Andrew Jr.
Johnson, Carl E.
Johnson, Charles B.
Johnson, Charlie A.
Johnson, Clarence
Johnson, Conrad A., Jr.
Johnson, Earl C.
Johnson, Langdon E.
Johnson, Louis W.
Johnson, Robert M.
Johnson, Rupert C.
Johnson, Theopolis W.
Johnson, Wilbert H.
Johnston, William A., Jr.
Jones, Beecher A.
Jones, Edgar L.
Jones, Frank D.

Jones, Hubert L.
Jones, Major E.
Jones, Robert Jr.
Jones, William M.
Jordan, Lowell H.
Keel, Daniel
Keith, Laurel E.
Kelley, Thomas A.
Kelly, Earl
Kennedy, Elmore M.
Kennedy, James V., Jr.
Kenney, Oscar A.
Kimbrough, Benny R.
King, Celestus
King, Earl E.
King, Haldane
Kirkpatrick, Felix J.
Kirksey, LeRoy
Knight, Calvin M.
Knight, Frederick D., Jr.
Knight, William H.
Knighten, James B.
Knox, George L.
Kydd, George H. III
Lacy, Hezekiah
Laird, Edward
Lanauze, Harry E.
Lancaster, Theodore W.
Lane, Allen G.
Lane, Charles A., Jr.
Lane, Earl R.
Langston, Carroll N. Jr.
Lanham, Jimmy
Lankford, Joshua J Jr
Lawrence, Erwin B.
Lawrence, Robert W.
Lawson, Herman A.
Lawson, Walter Irving
Leahr, John H.
Lee, Frank
Leftenant, Samuel G.
Leftwich, Ivey L.
Leonard, Wilmore B.
Leslie, William A.
Lester, Clarence D.
Lewis, Herbert Jr.
Lewis, Joe A.
Lewis, William R.
Lieteau, Albert J.
Liggins, Wayne V.
Lindsey, Perry W.
Lockett, Claybourne A.
Long, Clyde C., Jr
Long, Wilbur F.
Love, Thomas W., Jr.
Lucas, Wendell M.
Lyle, John H.
Lyle, Payton H.

Lynch, George A.
Lynch, Lewis J.
Lynn, Samuel
Macon, Richard D.
Manley, Edward E.
Mann, Hiram E.
Manning, Albert H.
Manning, Walter P.
Manson, Ralph W.
Maples, Andrew Jr.
Maples, Harold B.
Marshall, Andrew D.
Martin, August J.
Martin, Maceo C., Jr.
Martin, Robert L.
Masciana, Andrea P.
Mason, James W.
Mason, Theodore O.
Mason, Vincent J.
Matthews, Charles R.
Matthews, George B.
Matthews, Samuel
Mattison, William T.
Maxwell, Charles C.
Maxwell, Robert L.
May, Cornelius F.
McCarroll, Rixie H.
McClelland, Harvey L.
McClenic, William B.
McClure, John W.
McCreary, Walter L.
McCrory, Felix M.
McCrumby, George T.
McCullin, James L.
McDaniel, Armour G.
McGarrity, Thomas H.
McGee, Charles E.
McGinnis, Faythe A.
McIntyre, Clinton E.
McIntyre, Herbert A.
McIver, Frederick D., Jr.
McKeethen, Lloyd B.
McKenzie, Alfred U.
McKnight, James W.
McLaurin, Eddie A.
McQuillan, Douglas H.
McRae, Ivan J., Jr.
Melton, William R., Jr.
Merriweather, Robert O.
Merriwether, Elbert Jr.
Merton, Joseph L., Jr.
Miller, Charles E.
Miller, George R.
Miller, Godfrey C.
Miller, Lawrence I.
Miller, Oliver O.
Miller, Willard B.
Millett, Joseph H.

Mills, Clinton B.
Mills, Theodore H.
Mitchell, James T., Jr.
Mitchell, Paul G.
Mitchell, Vincent I.
Moffett, Wilbur
Moody, Frank H.
Moody, Paul L.
Moody, Roland W.
Moore, Abe B.
Moore, Flarzell
Moore, Theopolis D.
Moore, Willis E.
Moret, Calvin G.
Morgan, Dempsey W.
Morgan, John H.
Morgan, William B.
Morgan, Woodrow F.
Morris, Harold M.
Morrison, Thomas J., Jr.
Moseley, Sidney J.
Mosley, Clifford E.
Mosley, John W.
Moss, Richard M.
Mozee, David M., Jr.
Mulzac, John I.
Murdic, Robert J.
Murphy, David J. Jr.
Murray, Louis U.
Myers, Charles P.
Nalle, Russell C., Jr.
Neblett, Nicholas S.
Nelson, Dempsey Jr.
Nelson, John W.
Nelson, Lincoln W.
Nelson, Neal V.
Nelson, Robert H., Jr.
Newman, Christopher W.
Newsum, Fitzroy
(H) Nicolas, Felissier C.
Nightingale, Elton H.
Noches, Ramon F.
Norton, George G., Jr.
Oliphant, Clarence A.
Oliver, Luther L.
O'Neal, Walter N.
O'Neil, Robert
Orduna, Ralph
Page, Maurice R.
Palmer, Augustus L.
Palmer, Walter J.
Parker, Frederick L.
Parker, George J.
Parker, Melvin
Parkey, Robert M.
(H) Pasquet, Alix
Patton, Humphrey C.

Patton, Thomas G.
Payne, Turner W.
Payne, Verdell L.
Peirson, Gwynne W.
Pendleton, Frederick D.
Penn, Sterling B.
Pennington, Leland H.
Pennington, Robert F.
Peoples, Francis B.
Peoples, Henry R.
Perkins, John R., Jr.
Perkins, Roscoe C., Jr
Perkins, Sanford M.
Perry, Henry B.
Pillow, Robert A., Jr.
Pinkney, Harvey N.
Polkinghorne, James R.
Pollard, Henry Jr.
Pompey, Maurice D.
Ponder, Driskell B.
Porter, Calvin V., Jr.
Porter, John H.
Porter, Robert B.
Powell, William S., Jr.
Prather, George L.
Prewitt, Mexion O.
Price, Charles R.
Price, William S. III
Prince, Joseph A.
Proctor, Norman E.
Proctor, Oliver W.
Prowell, John R.
Pruitt, Harry S.
Pruitt, Wendell O.
Pullam, Richard C.
Pulliam, Glenn W.
Purchase, Leon
Purnell, George B.
Purnell, Louis R.
Qualles, John P.
Quander, Charles J., Jr.
Radcliff, Lloyd L.
Ragsdale, Lincoln J.
Ramsey, James C.
Ramsey, Pierce T.
Rapier, Gordon M.
Rayburg, Nathaniel P.
Rayford, Lee
Raymond, Frank R.
Rayner, Ahmed A., Jr.
Rector, John A.
Reed, Marsille P.
Reeves, Ronald W.
Reid, Jr., Maury M.
Reynolds, Clarence E., Jr.
Rhodes, George M., Jr.
Rice, Clayo C.
Rice, Price D.

Rice, William E.
Rich, Daniel L.
Richardson, Eugene J., Jr.
Richardson, Virgil J.
Roach, Charles J.
Roach, John B.
Robbins, Emory L., Jr.
Roberts, Frank E.
Roberts, George S.
Roberts, Lawrence E.
Roberts, Leon C.
Roberts, LeRoy Jr.
Roberts, Logan
Robinson, Carroll H.
Robinson, Curtis C.
Robinson, Isaiah E., Jr.
Robinson, Robert C., Jr.
Robinson, Robert L., Jr.
Robinson, Spencer M. *
Robinson, Theodore W.
Robnett, Harris H., Jr.
Rodgers, Marion R.
Rogers, Amos A.
Rogers, Cornelius G.
Rogers, John W.
(V) Rohlsen, Henry E.
Romine, Roger
Ross, Mac
Ross, Merrill R.
Ross, Washington D.
Rowe, Claude A.
Rucker, William A.
Russell, James C.
Samuels, Frederick H.
Sanderlin, Willis E.
Satterwhite, Harry J.
Saunders, Martin G.
Saunders, Pearlee E.
Sawyer, Harold E.
Scales, Norman W.
Schell, Wyrian T.
Schwing, Herbert J.
Scott, Floyd R.
Scott, Henry B.
Scott, Joseph P.
Scott, Wayman E.
Selden, Wiley W.
Sessions, Mansfield L.
Sheats, George H.
Shepherd, James H.
Sheppard, Harry A.
Sherard, Earl S., Jr.
Sherman, George
Shivers, Clarence L.
Shults, Lloyd R.
Sidat-Singh, Wilmeth W.
Simeon, Albert B., Jr.
Simmons, Alfonso

Simmons, Donehue
Simmons, Paul C.
Simons, Richard A.
Simpson, Jesse H.
Singletary, Lloyd G.
Sloan, John S.
Smith, Albert H.
Smith, Burl E.
Smith, Edward N.
Smith, Eugene D.
Smith, Frederick D.
Smith, Graham
Smith, Harold E., Jr.
Smith, Lewis C.
Smith, Luther H.
Smith, Quentin P.
Smith, Reginald V.
Smith, Robert C.
Smith, Robert H.
Smith, Thomas W.
Spann, Calvin J.
Spears, Leon W.
Spencer, Roy M.
Spicer, Cecil
Spriggs, Thurman E.
Spurlin, Jerome D.
Squires, John W.
Stanton, Charles R.
Starks, Arnett W., Jr.
Stephenson, William Jr.
Stevens, Richard G.
Steward, Lowell C.
Stewart, Harry T., Jr.
Stewart, Nathaniel C.
Stiger, Roosevelt
Stoudmire, Norvell
Stovall, Charles L.
Streat, William A., Jr.
Street, Thomas C.
Suggs, John J.
Surcey, Wayman P.
Talton, James E.
Tate, Charles W.
Taylor, Elmer W.
Taylor, George A.
Taylor, James H.
Taylor, Ulysses S.
Taylor, William H., Jr.
Temple, Alva N.
Terry, Kenneth E.
Terry, Roger C.
Theodore, Eugene G.
Thomas, Edward M.
Thomas, Walter H., Jr.
Thomas, William H.
Thompson, Donald N., Jr.
Thompson, Floyd A.
Thompson, Francis R.

Thompson, James A.
Thompson, Reid E.
Thorpe, Herbert C.
Thorpe, Richard E.
Tindall, Thomas J.
Toatley, Ephraim E.
Tompkins, William D.
Toney, Mitchel N.
Toppins, Edward L.
Tresville, Robert B., Jr.
Trott, Robert G.
Tucker, Paul
Turner, Allen H.
Turner, Andrew D.
Turner, Gordon G.
Turner, John B.
Turner, Leon L.
Turner, Leonard F.
Turner, Ralph L.
Twine, Saint M.
Tyler, William A., Jr.
Valentine, Cleophus W.
Vaughn, Leonard O.
Velasquez, Frederick E.
Verwayne, Peter C.
Waddell, Reginald C., Jr.
Walker, Charles E.
Walker, Frank D.
Walker, James A.
Walker, John B., Jr.
Walker, Quitman C.
Walker, William C., Jr.
Walker, William H.
Walker, William H.
Wanamaker, George E.
Warner, Hugh St. Clair
Warren, James W.
Warrick, Calvin T.
Washington, Milton S.
Washington, Morris J.
Washington, Samuel L.
Washington, William M.
Watkins, Edward W.
Watkins, Edward W., Jr.
Watson, Dudley M.
Watson, Spann
Watts, Samuel W., Jr.
Weatherford, Richard
Weathers, Luke J.
Webb, Rhohelia J.
Wells, Johnson C.
Wells, Wendell D.
Westbrook, Shelby F.
Westmoreland, Julius C.
Westmoreland, Walter D.
Wheeler, Jimmie D.
Wheeler, William M.
White, Charles L.

White, Cohen M.
White, Ferrier H.
White, Harold L.
White, Harry W.
White, Haydel J.
White, Hugh J.
White, Joseph C.
White, Marvin C., Jr
White, Raymond M.
White, Sherman W.
White, Vertner J., Jr.
Whitehead, John L., Jr.
Whiten, Joseph P.
Whiteside, Albert Jr.
Whitney, Yenwith K.
Whittaker, Peter H.
Whyte, James W., Jr.
Wiggins, Leonard W.
Wiggins, Robert H.
Wilburn, Arthur J.
Wiley, James T.
Wilhite, Emmet J.
Wilkerson, Oscar L.
Wilkerson, William G.
Wilkins, Lawrence D.
Wilkins, Ralph D.
Willette, Leonard R.
Williams, Andrew B., Jr.
Williams, Charles I.
Williams, Charles T.
Williams, Clarence
Williams, Craig H.
Williams, Edward J.
Williams, Eugene W.
Williams, Herbert J.
Williams, James L.
Williams, James R.
Williams, Joseph H.
Williams, Kenneth I.
Williams, LeRoi S.
Williams, Leslie A.
Williams, Raymond L.
Williams, Robert E., Jr.
Williams, Robert W.
Williams, Romeo M.
Williams, Thomas E.
Williams, Vincent E.
Williams, William F.
Williams, William L. Jr.
Williams, Yancey
Williamson, Willie A.
Wilson, Bertram W., Jr.
Wilson, Charles E.
Wilson, James A.
Wilson, Leroy J.
Wilson, Myron
Wilson, Theodore A.
Winslow, Eugene

Winslow, Robert W.
Winston, Charles H.
Winston, Harry P.
Wise, Henry A., Jr.
Wofford, Kenneth O.
Woods, Carl J.
Woods, Carrol S.
Woods, Isaac R.
Woods, Willard L.
Wooten, Howard A.
Wright, Frank N.
Wright, Hiram
Wright, James W., Jr.
Wright, Kenneth M.
Wright, Sandy W., Jr
Wyatt, Beryl
Wynn, Nasby
Yates, Phillip C.
York, Oscar H.
Young, Albert L.
Young, Benjamin Jr.
Young, Eddie L.
Young, Leo W.
Young, William W.

Sources of Photographs

NOTE: All images not specifically credited in the list below were provided courtesy of the authors.

Abbreviations used:

AFHRA: Air Force Historical Research Agency, Maxwell AFB, AL collection

AUHO: Air University Office of History

BWE: Black Wings Exhibit and Book Collection, National Air and Space Museum Acc. No. 1992-0060

CRL: Col Roosevelt J. Lewis (USAF, Ret) collection, Moton Field, Tuskegee, Alabama

DVIC: Defense Visual Information Center collection

NARA: National Archives and Records Administration collection

NASM: National Air and Space Museum, Smithsonian Institution

OCAMF: Octave Chanute Aerospace Museum Foundation

PTS: Pilot Training School, Tuskegee Institute

Page 16 (far left), BWE. 18 (top), BWE. 18 (bottom), NASM. 20, NASM. 28 (top left, top right), PTS. 32, PTS. 33 (top, bottom), PTS. 35 (top, bottom), PTS. 36 (top, bottom), PTS. 37 (top, bottom), PTS. 45 (bottom), PTS. 48 (bottom), PTS. 49 (top, middle, bottom), PTS. 50 (bottom), PTS. 51 (top, bottom), PTS. 52 (top), PTS. 56 (top), NARA. 61 (top), AUHO. 68, AFHRA. 70, PTS. 72, CRL. 76 (top), NARA. 80 (top), AFHRA. 81 (top, bottom), CRL. 82 (middle, bottom), PTS. 84, PTS. 85 (top), PTS. 87 (top, middle, bottom), OCAMF. 88 (bottom), OCAMF. 89 (bottom), OCAMF. 92 (top, bottom), OCAMF. 93, CRL. 95, NARA. 102, NARA. 104 (top), CRL. 105 (top, bottom), NARA. 106 (top, bottom), NARA. 107 (top), AUHO. 107 (bottom), NARA. 108 (top), NARA. 108 (bottom), AUHO. 109 (top, bottom), AUHO. 110 (top), CRL. 110 (bottom), NARA. 111, NARA. 112 (top, bottom), NARA. 113, NARA. 115 (top, bottom), AUHO. 116, CRL. 117 (top, bottom), CRL. 118 (top), AUHO. 118 (bottom), CRL. 119 (top, bottom), CRL. 121, CRL. 122, CRL. 123, CRL. 124 (top), CRL. 124 (bottom), NARA. 125 (top, bottom), NARA. 130, CRL. 132, OCAMF. 134, CRL. 135, CRL. 143 (bottom), NASM. 145 (top), NARA. 145 (bottom), DVIC. 146 (top), OCAMF. 147 (top, bottom), OCAMF. 148 (top, bottom), OCAMF. 149 (top, bottom), DVIC. 150 (top, bottom), DVIC. 153, Department of Defense photograph by Scott M. Ash, U.S. Air Force. 155, PTS. 156, PTS. 159, PTS. 188, CRL. 203, Air Warfare Center, Nellis AFB, Nevada, collection. 204 (bottom), AFHRA.

Acknowledgments

The authors acknowledge the invaluable assistance that others provided them in the production of this book. Thanks to the owners of NewSouth Books, Randall Williams and Suzanne La Rosa, and members of their staff, including Jeff Benton, Brian Seidman, Kelsey Loftin, Lisa Harrison, Sam Robards, Noelle Matteson, Nichole Peacock, and Lisa Emerson.

Charles O'Connell, director of the Air Force Historical Research Agency, allowed the authors to spend much time working on the book project, and other members of the agency provided crucial help, including archivist Sylvester Jackson, who found and identified photographs and documents, and Ronald Myers, head of the accessions division of the agency, who collected many of the electronic versions of the photographs.

Dr. Wesley P. Newton provided encouragement and expertise on local Tuskegee Airmen.

Members of the Tuskegee Airmen Incorporated provided research assistance, including members of its Harry A. Sheppard historical research committee. Among them was the late William Holloman, an original Tuskegee Airman who served as head of the committee, and George Hardy, another original Tuskegee Airman who replaced Holloman when he passed away in 2010. Other members included Alexander Jefferson, another original Tuskegee Airman, and researchers Craig Huntly and Robert Iversen, who contributed their discoveries among the documents.

William Holton, who served as the national historian of the Tuskegee Airmen Incorporated from 1997–2007, provided valuable historical insights, as did the current national historian, Zellie Orr. For some of the photographs, the authors acknowledge the work of Roosevelt Lewis, former director of Moton Field at Tuskegee, and Air Education and Training Command historians Richard J. Burkard and Richard H. Emmons.

Others, too numerous to name, also contributed to this very important story.

Index

About the Authors

JOSEPH CAVER is a senior archivist at the Air Force Historical Research Agency at Maxwell Air Force Base in Montgomery, Alabama. His article "Setting the Record Straight Regarding Lieutenants White and McCullin, Tuskegee Airmen," written with Jerome Ennels and Wesley Newton and published in the 2008 *Air Power History Journal*, was selected as the article of the year by the *Journal*. He received the 2010 Spirit of Marion Award from Alabama State University.

JEROME ENNELS is a former Air University Historian and currently an archivist at the Air Force Historical Research Agency. Mr. Ennels has published numerous unit histories, monographs, studies, and articles in newspapers and professional journals. He is the co-author with Wesley Newton of *The Wisdom Of Eagles: A History of Maxwell Air Force Base*.

DANIEL L. HAULMAN is Chief, Organizational History Division, at the Air Force Historical Research Agency, where he has worked since 1982. He has authored three books, including *Air Force Aerial Victory Credits: World War I, World War II, Korea, and Vietnam*; *The United States and Air Force and Humanitarian Airlift Operations, 1947–1994*; and *One Hundred Years of Flight: USAF Chronology of Significant Air and Space Events, 1903–2002*.